EAST OF TIME
Jacob G. Rosenberg

T0288190

JACOB G. ROSENBERG was born in Lodz, Poland, the youngest member of a working-class family. After the Germans occupied Poland he was confined, with his parents, his two sisters and their little girls, to the Lodz Ghetto, from which they were eventually transported to Auschwitz. Except for one sister (who committed suicide a few days later) all the members of his family were gassed on the day of their arrival. He remained in Auschwitz for about two months, then spent the rest of the war in other concentration camps. In 1948 he emigrated to Australia with his wife Esther; their only child, Marcia, was born in Melbourne. Rosenberg's poems and stories have appeared both in Australia and overseas. He has published three books of poetry in English, as well as three earlier volumes of prose and poetry in Yiddish. This is his second book of prose in English.

ALSO BY JACOB G. ROSENBERG

Poetry and prose in Yiddish
Snow in Spring
Wooden Clogs Shod with Snow
Light — Shadow — Light

Poetry in English
My Father's Silence
Twilight Whisper
Elegy on Ghetto (*video*)
Behind the Moon

Prose in English
Lives and Embers

East of Time

Jacob G. Rosenberg

THE UNIVERSITY OF ALABAMA PRESS
Tuscaloosa

Copyright © 2005
Jacob G. Rosenberg

Published 2007 by The University of Alabama Press
Tuscaloosa, Alabama 35487-0380

First published in Australia by Brandl & Schlesinger, Book Publishers.

Rosenberg, Jacob G., 1922-
East of time
"Fire Ant books"

ISBN-13 978-0-8173-5449-7 (pbk. : alk. paper)
ISBN-10 0-1873-5449-2 (pbk. : alk. paper)

Cataloging-in-publication data available from the Library of Congress.

For Marcia, with love

ACKNOWLEDGMENTS

I wish to express my deep appreciation to my editor, Alex Skovron, who like a biblical scribe has led me through three collections of poetry and now two books of prose. I am convinced that thanks to him the gods of literature are watching over me.

My heartfelt gratitude to Professor Louis Waller and Professor Richard Freadman, and to Alex Miller, for giving so generously of their time, reading the manuscript, and offering valued comments and responses.

I want also to thank Bernard Hirsch for his scriptural counsel.

Finally, I am indebted yet again to my dear Esther, who constantly dispels my often self-imposed disenchantments.

East of Time is a rendezvous of history and imagination, of realities and dreams, of hopes and disenchantments. The story is set in Łódź (Lodz), city of the waterless river, the Łódka, which in my time consisted largely of black mud from the town's industrial waste. Thanks to its mighty textile industry, the city was known as the Polish Manchester. My rendezvous spans a period from childhood to early maturity, a period when I witnessed the grand belief in a just new world overtaken, first, by the cataclysmic events of the 1930s, then incarcerated between the walls of the ghetto established in my town by the Germans, and finally silenced at Auschwitz.

The anecdotes, incidents and characters that appear throughout these pages come directly from my memories — although some names have been changed, and occasionally I have succumbed to the story-teller's prerogative (and delight) in a measure of embellishment, not to say invention. The narrative is broadly if not slavishly chrono-logical, with brief excursions where appropriate into the future or the past. The touchstone of these reminiscences — their informing spirit — is the desire and determination of an entire community to remain human, even at the last frontier of life.

The short verses quoted here and there are the songs and poems of the people of my world — an intimate, inseparable part of the human landscape of the times, and a defiant response to the adversities of daily existence.

As for the many individuals who populate this book, most, with one or two exceptions, are now dead, murdered during those years of darkness. Some readers may question my purpose in summoning up all these names, but the need to recall them is strong within me; perhaps it is the scriptural influence, or maybe the voice of my forefathers, to whom the mentioning of names was a sacred duty.

J.G.R.

✎ *Bona Fides* ✎

I was born to the east of time, in the city of a waterless river, in a one-room palace. My parents were millionaires: father was a textile weaver of dreams, mother was a spinner. My two sisters and I shuttled between the threads of their colourful yarns.

With the break of dawn my father and mother rushed off to work (if there was work), my sisters to school, and I to the nearby kindergarten. I was always the first one there. Alone in the big playroom, I watched the dance of shadows, touched the terror of emptiness, and listened to the drumming of the loose windowpanes in the wind.

At the age of seven I became a student at the unique Vladimir Medem school, a private establishment owned by an ideology, that of the socialist Bund. But a fee still had to be paid, so father forever went about in second-hand suits and shoes — education for his children took precedence. At the school I was taught Yiddish and Polish, history, geography, mathematics, algebra, astronomy, and (most important) how to be a *mensch*. I passed well in most subjects but the last, in which my marks were low.

My teachers were mentors by day, librarians at dusk, and camp-leaders during our holidays. I loved them all, especially

Miss Joskowicz, a tall blonde who taught us Polish history, which I was very fond of. And although I was attentive to every word that emerged through her wholesome cherry lips, I never quite gained the grades I deserved. My father couldn't understand why. How could I explain to this straitlaced weaver, with dreams so different from mine, that between me and the subject I adored stood my beautiful teacher's majestic bosom, for which I was ready to give up not only the Polish kings but the royalty of the whole wide world?

There were no flowers in our secular schoolyard, no greenery in its vicinity. Amid a forest of red chimneys, with their luscious curly grey wigs of smoke, in a rented chain of rooms on the third floor, under a lease of constant eviction, we feasted on magic gardens planted by devoted scribes in the singing pages of our Yiddish books.

My teachers, scholars in their own right, banned from universities for being Jewish, wore battered shoes and tattered shirts in our unheated rooms as they released Prometheus from his shackles, conquered the Sisyphean nightmare, then led us upon excursions to the heights of Kilimanjaro and the depths of the human soul.

Our unemployed fathers, whose days were too long and nights too short to bespeak and plan the glorious world to come, kept the school alive with their meagre earnings. Our down-to-earth mothers, serving hot barley soup for breakfast at break of dawn, hummed with all their heart Yitzhak Katzenelson's sunset songs:

My sun sinks into flames
On a dying beam;
Such is my hope,
My dream.

And my pale-faced companions with dark storytelling eyes readily confided, 'In our house, bread never gets the chance to go stale.'

Bałuty, where we lived, was the poorest quarter in our city. In this world of meek rebellious shoeless cobblers, coatless tailors and coughing miners, we were taught that there is no God. But that one ought to live one's life as if there is.

❧ My Father ❧

I'm no psychologist, but I would dare to guess that the path leading to a simple man's mind and heart is a straight one. My father Gershon was no simple man, perhaps because there were too many struggles and disappointments in his formative years. These made him the hopeful doubter, the optimistic pessimist that he was.

At the age of fourteen he was forced to leave his parents' home, his yeshiva life, the shtetl of his birth, and he arrived unexpected in the big city of the waterless river, where his older brother Avraham had established a textile factory in his dining-room. Father quickly learnt the trade, and after one year was already earning a rouble a week — which was collected for him by his sister-in-law, for 'safekeeping'.

The year 1905 was one of great proletarian ferment; strikes broke out, barricades were erected. The Russian masses had awoken, and Jewish workers, too, under the banner of the illegal Bund (of which my father was a leader), took to the streets with red flags, songs and placards demanding freedom, justice and better pay.

The ill-advised Tsar answered with bullets, and with persecution and pogroms against the Jews. My father was in the midst of it all. It was the spring of his life, he was young, a smallish but handsome man, with a song in his bones.

O brothers, we are united
Of life and death one band
Arm in arm dedicated
The red flag fast in our hand.

Should a bullet hit you, my true one
A bullet from our foe the hound
I'll carry you out from the fire
And heal with kisses your wound.

But if you fall in battle, my true one
And the light in your eyes is no more
I'll enfold you in our flag, the red one
And together we'll fight our war.

Two years later, in 1907, one evening just before dinner, there was a knock on the door of my father's unlit room. He opened it, and there they stood: two members of the notorious Ochrana, the Tsarist secret police. 'Gershon,' they said, 'you come with us.'

Gershon was sentenced to life in the freezing snows of Siberia. But the party hadn't forgotten him. Eighteen months later he escaped, having received false papers that entitled him to enter America. He got as far as Berlin, but here he began to doubt. If people like him started taking off, who would be left to make the revolution?

In 1913, Gershon married my beautiful hardworking mother, Masha. Were they suited? Were they happy? I don't know. Children, especially when their parents are long dead, like to think that everything in their mother and father's life together was smooth sailing. But Gershon was too restless a man to be fully satisfied with domestic bliss; he was still much involved in politics and the camaraderie of party life.

Yet when our world crumbled, when our springs arrived in a vortex of snow, and our summers walked about the earth in a mantle of dull dust, Gershon stood fast by his wife. Hand in hand he went with her, through the bleakest tunnel and to its very end, to the night that awaited them there.

≋ *My Mother* ≋

There was once a man of great piety, very few words, and many good deeds. His name was Aba and he fathered five daughters. One of them was my mother. Though she had a religious upbringing, she married a man who had totally abandoned all religious traditions. At first she still fostered some customs, such as candle-lighting, to which my father did not object; but since he was intellectually dominant, mother gradually fell under his spell. She joined his party, spoke his tongue, sang his songs, and began reading books, lots of books. Did this transformation bring happiness to her life? I don't know, it's hard to say — not because her son didn't often sense her resigned mood, her well-concealed melancholy, but because the phenomenon we call happiness is so difficult to define. In any case, all her qualities — including that of being physically stronger than father, and (because of her skill level) an earner he could never hope to be — made mother an equal partner in my parents' marriage.

I cannot remember my mother not singing, though again there was a sadness in her voice, a sadness that could transform even a simple folksong into a tender psalm:

> *Childhood, beautiful childhood years*
> *In my memory forever you'll stay;*
> *When I think of you my eyes fill with tears,*
> *Oh, how quickly my childhood flew away.*

These psalm-songs were my mother's cocoon, where she could hide, feel safe, and feel whole.

I knew that mother loved her husband deeply, but I doubt if her love was returned in the same measure. There was a disparity in my parents' life. Mother's world was her home; father's home was the world.

Mother was open with her children, especially with my sister Pola. One evening, when Pola was about twenty, mother said to her: 'You were born at the outbreak of the Great War. When I had you I was quite alone. Father continued with all his activities as if still a bachelor — he often attended long party meetings and discussions, and on a Saturday or Sunday, after an all-day conference, he would go to the cinema with female comrades. I was hurt,' she confided, 'though I knew he wasn't being unfaithful.'

'*How* did you know, Mama?' asked my sister with tears in her eyes. 'How did you know?'

'Because when he came back, his lovemaking was always more intense than ever… Though even then,' mother added in a whisper, 'he was selfish.'

'Then why didn't you leave him?' her daughter cried.

'Because I love him with every fibre of my being. Love-making, dear child, is not love. Love is much, much more. Much, much more,' she repeated.

As daylight began to wane, a serenity that almost glowed would settle on mother's face. Her moist brown eyes would glisten, and though she did not move her lips, I knew that everything in her was singing, singing its way back into her cocoon, where my mother's darkening horizon could succumb to the music of her inner light:

O little Sabbath candles,
Your flames an everlasting story;
My father's home,
My people's glory.

❧ An Incident ❧

One summer, mother and I went for a short vacation on a villager's farm, about ten kilometres from our city of the water-less river. On a sunny, still afternoon, mother, the most beautiful woman in the whole world (I was six at the time), wearing a pale-blue linen dress trimmed with gilded buttons, spread a chequered red woollen blanket on a lush patch of grass, sprinkled with wildflowers, not far from the farm. As we were about to sit down, a pleasant-looking man — one Mr Wolf, a friend from mother's younger years who happened to know that we had arrived — came over to say hello.

Mr Wolf had a ruddy face and shiny black hair parted in the middle; he wore white slacks, a navy-blue shirt and a pair of gold-rimmed sunglasses. Uninvited, he stretched himself on the edge of our blanket and, chewing on a blade of grass, began to murmur to mother under his breath. Mother smiled and smiled, but wouldn't answer him. He turned up again the next day, and the next. On the third day, mother weakened and responded to his murmurs with half-words that I couldn't understand. When he finally left us, I asked her who this man was and what he wanted. She replied that he was just a wandering pleasure-seeker. What did that mean, I wanted to know. A funny and harmless adventurer, she explained.

Later that afternoon, when we returned to the small room we were renting at the farm, mother asked the farmer for some roses. As she placed them in a vase, I heard her say to herself: 'The riper the rose, the nastier the bug.'

The following morning we cut short our little holiday. Thinking back, I wonder if it was because my resolute mother feared Mr Wolf... No, I don't think so. What she probably feared more was herself.

➮ *My Sister Pola* ➮

Are we not the rightful heirs of our parents' virtues and blemishes, the beneficiaries of their spiritual genes? And are we not also infected by the social and political bacteria of our time? My sister Pola was born in the shadow of the Great War, of formidable public upheavals, pogroms, and the Russian Revolution.

At age sixteen, in the city of the waterless river, she joined the KZM, the Communist Union of Youth. Our father, the anti-Communist labour man, was visibly upset. I was present when he spoke to her about the fate of those who fought for her cause, years before Arthur Koestler immortalized N.S. Rubashov in *Darkness at Noon*. But my mercurial sister refused to be deterred by father's grim warnings. 'Anti-Soviet garbage!' she fired back. She produced from her bag a coloured flyer with a picture of a young, happily smiling *Komsomolec*, whom she dreamt to emulate. '*This* is the truth about the Soviet Union,' she shouted triumphantly. 'Anything else is just Fascist propaganda.' 'Who taught you that,' father asked quietly, 'your cell leader?' 'Yes,' she replied. 'In fact, he has just returned from Moscow.' Father shook his head. 'Well, my daughter,' he said, 'as it is written, you would do well to keep your distance from a fool, so that you don't learn foolish talk.'

At eighteen, Pola was arrested and sentenced to three years in prison for encouraging the workers of Poznanski's textile factory to down their tools, and for distributing leaflets with the following text:

O worker, brother, awake, awake,
See how the east has banished the night;
Comrade Stalin has ignited the flame
And restored to glory your right.

But nothing could discourage my doughty sister from
her task. When, at her trial, she was asked her religion, she
answered resolutely: 'None!' Did she have anything to say in
her defence, the judge inquired. 'Yes, your honour. I have been
beaten in prison. That's illegal!' The judge ordered her taken
away; Pola went on screaming, 'It's illegal, it's illegal!' For her
audacity she received from the court policeman two hefty
slaps across her face. She bled, mother fainted; but Pola would
not be silenced.

Not long after her release from prison, she married — but
the wrong man, who would soon abandon her to save his own
skin. And as she was celebrating her little daughter's fourth
birthday, the Great Leader, the one who had set the east
aflame and for whom she would gladly have died, went into
partnership with the arch-enemy of humanity.

Five years later, in a dark cattle-train headed for Auschwitz, I heard Pola sing a lullaby to her sobbing little girl:

Sleep, my darling Frumetl,
Close your dreamy eyes;
Where the lilacs blossom
Are bluer skies…

Little Frumetl was gassed on arrival.

Betrayed by the man she loved, and by the party she
served, Pola left her barrack at midnight and, with arms out-
stretched as if in supplication, embraced the buzzing wires of
Birkenau's electric fence.

❧ My Sister Ida ❧

There was something contradictory about my sister Ida. On the one hand, she was a quiet, unassuming, polite little girl; on the other, a restless, frolicking child, mischievous almost to the extreme. Her history and literature teacher, Yuda Reznik, once told father, presumably in jest: 'If you won't take her out of school, I'm going to kill myself.' Perhaps, like all the girls in her class, my sister was in love with this charismatic man.

Ida was of slender build but well-shaped, with a wave of auburn hair that danced alluringly over her forehead, her black eyebrows and her deep brown eyes. She carried herself with a pleasing, lingering quietude. Ida passed through our shadowy world like a pale ray of some mysterious hope. But every mystery conceals a story.

She was only fifteen, and just three months from obtaining her school certificate, when her sister Pola's marital life ran into difficulties. Putting aside her own needs and feelings, Ida left the school she loved and her friends there to look after Pola's two-year-old infant girl.

After that, life took a new turn.

Young men were readily attracted to Ida. At the outbreak of war in 1939, as booted hordes from the west descended on the country of my birth, there was the young fine-looking carpenter, the Bundist Grinszpan, who loved her dearly and begged her to run away with him to the east. But Ida shook her head. 'No,' she told him. 'I wouldn't leave mother behind.'

Of course, there were plenty of others — among them a fellow who, if not too prudent, was certainly persistent. He kept hanging around, endeared himself to our mother, and finally found a place in my sister's heart. Possibly this changed the course of her life. I know that one shouldn't point the finger, that life is serendipitous; that he who guards his tongue (as it is written) guards himself from evil. Nonetheless, I believe there are times when even the cruellest truth is preferable to the gentlest lie.

When Ida became pregnant she was barely twenty-two years old. I still recall the duel of eyes as she broke the news to mother, and then father's blunt but pragmatic remark: 'It's not too late…' For quite a few days, the spirit of the Pharaoh who didn't know Joseph struggled against the spirit of Shifra and Puah. Obviously, however, a foetus was not a sufficient offering to our Almighty — He desired much more.

I vividly remember the unlit carriage of a screaming cattle-train, and Ida hushing her whining little Chayale to sleep:

There once was a king,
There once was a page,
There once was a beautiful queen…

The lullaby told of the terrible death that befell the royal threesome: the king was eaten by a dog, the page by a cat, and the queen by a little mouse! But the child should not grieve, the song concluded — for the king was made of sugar, the page of gingerbread, and the queen was of marzipan…

We arrived at our destination on a hot August day of barking dogs. There, beneath an unblemished sky, dressed in black and with gloves of white, stood a man called Mengele who was convinced that he was God's deputy.

≈ *Legends* ≈

Berta Winograd was my form and geography teacher. Nick-named 'Petcha', she was a tiny green-eyed brunette, with a scorch mark on her right cheek from an accident while still a child. Berta always wore a black tight-fitting dress and a string of white pearls around her neck. She was in her early thirties, unmarried, came from a wealthy family, and rumour had it that she refused to be paid for her work. (School-children often know more about their teachers than about their own parents.)

A million years have flown by since my schooldays, yet time has not erased from my memory Berta's excursions into fantastic landscapes, where we encountered exotic peoples, learnt about their customs and listened to their tales — without leaving our classroom. Berta was a granary of vivid legends. Legends, she would say, were not bedtime stories or lullabies, but evocative fables — echoes of what was real. They were a kind of poetry you had to know how to read, how to interpret allegorically, in order to penetrate their meaning and enrich your life.

During the fifth year of my studies, in the third month of the year, on the second day of the week, Berta, who never needed to raise her voice to quieten her students, made her way into the classroom with a strange, almost secretive expression on her face. I was thirteen at the time, yet I haven't forgotten — or am imagining that I remember — the green glint in her eyes, her measured walk, the blend of dignity and mystery she projected.

'The philosopher Chuang Tzu,' Berta began, 'dreamt that he was a butterfly. When he awoke, he didn't know whether he was a man who had dreamt he was a butterfly, or a butterfly that was dreaming it was a man.'

Suddenly the door opened. Our nervous principal, accompanied by a bald inspector who kept harassing our school, looking for excuses to close it down, burst into the classroom. 'And what are we teaching here today?' sneered the representative of the government's education board, which regarded our school as a nest of future subversives.

'The humanity of a butterfly,' Berta replied in a whisper.

'Hm,' said the educator. 'Perhaps we should try something else — mathematics, for instance. Students! Pencils in hand, open your exercise books,' the intruder ordered. 'Now, given that there are 360 degrees of longitude, and fifteen of these equal one hour, what time would it be in Moscow, if it is twelve noon in London?'

The class froze: I could taste the tension on my tongue. Then, almost in unison, a forest of twenty young hands shot up to answer the challenge. All of them had the correct answer! The inspector could scarcely conceal his astonishment.

Berta, discreetly removing a white lace handkerchief from her sleeve, managed to stop a tear of triumphant joy from falling to the floor.

⇜ *Phantasm* ⇝

A certain mystery surrounded my teacher of natural science, 'Miss Lazar' Melman. Her olive skin, her pitch-black eyes, her Flamenco body-talk and her voice — like the rustling, silky pages of a book of psalms — betrayed, at least to me, a Marrano background, maybe even that of a royal Castilian.

One evening in March 1935, a group of five students, including me, were invited to the Melmans'. They lived a few doors from my family, in a sparsely decorated apartment, and we were meeting there to discuss our form's contribution to the forthcoming concert, 'The Dawn of Spring', a festive affair staged annually by the children of our school.

I was elated, convinced that my inclusion by Miss Lazar was no accident. Making my way to her door, I felt everything within me rejoicing. Perhaps she would permit me to sit next to her, to touch her arm — why not? Unfortunately my joy was shortlived. As I crossed her threshold I beheld a scene with which I simply could not come to terms. My teacher, the descendant of a possible Castilian prince, was a housewife, standing in her kitchen and cooking soup! To make matters worse, her husband, who taught Jewish Antiquity at our school and was known to his students by the uncomplimentary nickname 'Shmelke', shamelessly addressed her in the familiar second-person.

I believe Miss Lazar read my thoughts, for on the very next morning she managed to restore, in my eyes, her aristocratic Iberian image.

'Science,' began Donna Lazar, right at the start of her lesson, 'can both assist and destroy nature. Permit me, dear children,' she continued, looking directly at me, 'to illustrate this with an old Spanish folktale.

'There was once a young flower that grew in a village. It had not been cultivated in any garden and it grew on the fringes of the season, a startling indigo blossom. A curious scientist arrived to study it; he conducted some experiments to determine its character, but the flower soon withered away. Although this happened many, many years ago, the local peasants still swear that, come night, they can hear the flowers of the village weeping…'

I must admit that at the time I could not understand the fable. Much later, I realized that my teacher's story was a Ladino song of our past and our bygone future.

≈ *My First Poem* ≈

Spring in the city of the waterless river, where the grey had not yet displaced the blue. Rhythmic clatter of horses, their rich golden dung on the cobblestone roads. Rumble of iron-shod wheels on wooden carts laden with an abundance of farm produce. Gardens of budding lilac.

Enveloped in such evocative tranquillity, I made my solitary way to school. I was just a boy. How was I to know that all of this was but the transient smile of a landscape which was destined to pass from the world forever?

The morning's first lesson was poetry, a compulsory subject in our school. All students had to know the classics by heart. My Spanish lady, in her ever-tight white-cage blouse, entered the classroom in the company of a tall man wearing a black cape, a white linen shirt fastened with a burgundy cravat, and a grey fedora — which, as he took it off, released a black waterfall of curly hair that cascaded down over his high pale forehead.

'Children,' said my Castilian princess as we remained standing, 'I want you to meet the great poet, Moyshe Broderzon, who has agreed to talk to us about the art of writing prose and poetry.'

Although Broderzon addressed us in the simplest language, I am not sure if we — or at least I — grasped everything he said. 'Good writing,' he explained, 'is a meeting of heart and mind, of storm and calm. Here the sun may set and rise at the same time, a rose may blossom and instantly wither away. But always remember, children: the beauty of language is priceless, but never, ever, sacrifice wisdom on the altar of beautiful words.

'I once walked past a bronze statue,' Broderzon continued. 'It was the statue of a nameless poet. His face was like a letter in a lost tongue, and he stood there with his mouth open, as if needing more air. And on his pedestal was engraved the following short poem:

Youth is great and daring,
A stand against the world alone;
But a twig in a storm will outshine
A plant nursed quietly at home.'

That evening, while the flame in our kerosene lamp incited the shadows to wrestle, I secretly took my fountain-pen from my schoolbag, then watched as the ink began to flow. I wrote:

Three horses, three horses, white eagles,
Escaped the warmth of the king's stable
And flew into the face of the winds,
To dance in the heart of a fable.

At midnight, as the last ember died in our stove, my Spanish lady paid me a visit. With quivering hands she took my poem, and on her smile I erected a castle.

❧ *Awakening* ❧

Yuda Reznik, who taught me Yiddish literature, was a short man with thick curly hair and black laughing eyes. He always wore a skimpy tweed jacket which remembered his barmitzvah days, and a red tie that could have doubled as a shoelace. He was no saint, but one had to be blind not to see the halo of the song of I. L. Peretz about his head:

I'll swim around in the light
On a zephyr undisturbed;
Let no cloud obscure the sky
But the earth.

There wasn't a female student in our class who wasn't in love with him — and who could blame them, for he was a charmer. And a bridegroom of our language. There is more universality in Yiddish, he would say, than in Esperanto; more modernity in the old traditions than in the latest innovations. His comments on writing were phenomenal. Tell only half of what you know. Remember: a story without a shadow is a sad tale. It is not the first line of a story but the last which provokes the reader…

His lectures were a feast of poetry, mirage and fable. When he spoke, reality was vanquished and succumbed to myth, while reason won a Pyrrhic victory over emotion. Above all there was Peretz, father of modern Yiddish literature, who lived in every fibre of Reznik's being.

In 1939, as Europe reached a political boiling-point, as social democracy licked its wounds after the fall of the Spanish Republic; a day or two before the first of May, when we would celebrate international brotherhood (ours being a Bundist school), Reznik fronted the class in a new navy-blue jacket with the anti-Fascist badge on his lapel. He produced a book of working-class poetry and began to read. I cannot recall the poet's name but the last four lines of the poem are still with me:

Not far off is the time
Of freedom and of peace;
It may come late or soon —
That time is not a dream.

On a windy morning of a grey day in 1942, somewhere in the Polish city of Pinsk, a German rope would bring about Yuda Reznik's rude awakening.

❧ *The Violin* ❧

A professor of mathematics, a man who at times could be totally ignorant of the algebra of human feelings, was headmaster of our school — a school where the heart occupied the centre of all the disciplines. He lived a spartan life, his quarters a windowless cubicle somewhere among the rooms at the back. He'd never married, yet was never short of a wife.

I can scarcely remember him without a cigarette in his mouth, and a violin under his chin. He was a nervous man, a hard man, feared rather than liked. In his sleepless nights he composed medieval cloister melodies, morbid songs which he made us sing.

> *The skies are black with clouds,*
> *The trees the winds have torn;*
> *Where are you, my brother,*
> *Forsaken, forlorn?*

What happened to our headmaster was recounted to me years later by one of his students. After the war he had returned from the Siberian snows to his now desolate town, to his old lightless nook. He dropped his bundle of dry bones on the threadbare straw sack, and fell into a deep slumber.

Suddenly, as if in a dream, he heard the squeak of his door. When he opened his eyes he was surrounded by a group of strange individuals. 'Who are you, good people?' he asked in some alarm. 'What has brought you to me, an innocent teacher?'

For a good minute they stood there like men without tongues. Eventually one of them, the oldest, spoke. 'Sir,' he said, 'we are your former students, and we have brought back your lost violin.'

At this the spartan fell to his knees. Perhaps for the first time in his life, he found he could not hold back his tears. With quivering hands he accepted the instrument and placed it under his bony chin. And as his fingers began to dance like spider legs on the weeping strings, he invoked once again his descent into the darkness, the place where he felt most at home. At last he was free to explore the meaning of his wretched existence.

Then, all at once, he grew mortally pale. Pressing the fiddle firmly to his heart, he fell back on the straw sack. 'Thank you,' he said, 'thank you,' and closed his eyes for ever.

⇒ *Juda and the French Revolution* ⇒

At the age of fourteen my schoolmates, even before they had heard or read the history of the French Revolution, were a bunch of Jacobins, each of them a Gavroche at heart, with unequivocal belief in mankind's future and a boundless, passionate commitment to our common cause. So when our circle's political mentor, Juda Kersh, turned up on the fourteenth of July with a radiant face and a red carnation in his meagre lapel, his words to us were like a good fall of rain on fertile soil.

Juda was not what you might call an effervescent or exuberant man — perhaps the scholar in him dampened his spontaneity. He often spoke in a low tone, as if communing with himself, yet he had a marvellous way of inspiring his listeners, and an artful method of transforming events of the past into living experiences.

'In the last week of April, in the year 1789,' he began (Juda was also a fastidious historian, a great believer in dates), 'after a stern winter, a hungry destitute crowd of Parisians, en route to the National Assembly, found their march blocked by soldiers of the Royal-Cravate regiment. When they pelted the soldiers with stones, the latter responded with gunfire, and Paris had been baptised in its first river of blood.

'Yet it would be a mistake,' Juda continued, with his melancholy smile and his head tilted slightly to the right, 'to maintain that this incident, or various others like it, brought about the French Revolution. No, it was François Marie Arouet Voltaire's annihilating laughter and devastating irony, and Jean-Jacques Rousseau's sombre, sentimental primitivism, which pierced the heart of the rotten Bourbons, and consequently drove Paris to the barricades, where bayonet greeted bayonet, where in the bleeding streets the galvanized French masses, in their red, white and blue cockades, even as they died in battle beneath their red flags, triumphantly proclaimed—' here Juda rose to his full height and, in a voice quivering with emotion, cried out: '*Liberté, Égalité, Fraternité!*'

Upon this, he broke out in song:

> '*Allons enfants de la Patrie,*
> *Le jour de gloire est arrivé!*
> *Contre nous de la tyrannie,*
> *L'étendard sanglant est levé…*'

Then he stopped. 'And yet,' he said, the music still ringing in his voice, 'to my mind, it was not the words, but rather Rouget de Lisle's buoyant melody which became the beacon of light in men's darkest days.'

Many years later, in a dark ghetto basement, I noticed a green plant climbing a wet wall towards a tenuous crevice of sun. I don't know why, but I felt myself grow strangely tall, and at that moment I thought I spotted the phantom of Juda, his head tilted slightly to the right; and as he pointed his finger towards the struggling plant, the two of us began, simultaneously, to hum Rouget's eternal, resolute melody of hope.

❧ *Revolt* ❧

'The Dawn of Spring', as already mentioned, was an annual event at our school, a concert of musical and dramatic performances which involved the collective enterprise of students and teachers alike. I recall the year we staged *The Strike of the Hens*, a play based on a Sholem Aleichem story, 'Kapporos', meaning sacrifices. According to an old Babylonian custom, a day before Yom Kippur one ought to sacrifice a hen or a rooster, preferably a white one. Some believed that such an act would absolve that person's loved ones of their sins and safeguard their welfare for the coming year.

In Sholem Aleichem's story, just before Yom Kippur the hens, roosters and the whole poultry world proclaimed a strike. 'Enough!' they decided. 'Our life is ours, and we refuse to be sacrificed any longer for some people's fancy.' Well, our teachers quickly detected a sociopolitical moral in the tale; after some deliberation and rewriting, our surreal stage version of the story was born:

Officialdom (in our retelling) was beside itself at news of the strike, and a deputation was dispatched. 'What do you mean, you refuse to be sacrificed?' they bellowed. 'Who are you to challenge God's order, to take matters into your own hands?' An obese cleric in a black silk coat and fur cap came forward. 'Let *me* talk to them,' he told the delegation. 'I'll show them that anarchy cannot prevail, that everything on earth has been created with a purpose. Theirs is to be sacrificed and nothing will ever change that.'

But the rebellious poultry stood their ground. They sharpened their beaks on the wet blades of grass, ready to attack. Faced with this situation, the shrewd cleric modified his approach. 'My dear lady hens and honourable gentlemen roosters,' he coaxed. 'Please state your demands, and if they are within reason we can surely come to a settlement that will satisfy all concerned.'

A representative of the poultry fluttered to the front. 'We simply refuse to be your atonements,' she explained. 'We refuse to have our legs bound, to be spun around the heads of your sons and daughters, to be thrown under the table (as your stupid custom demands), and finally to be taken to the slaughterer, then cooked, fried or roasted to reappear on your white porcelain plates — and for what?'

'For what!' screamed the sweating cleric with the fur cap. 'Do you mean to say that the slaughterer's blessing as he cuts your throat is nothing? That *my* blessing before I sink my teeth into one of you young hens' juicy breasts is nothing?'

At this the multitude took a step forward. 'What sort of mockery is that?' they chorused. 'What sort of fools do you take us for?' Ruffling their feathers loudly, they formed a threatening phalanx. A young rooster pushed his way to the front and, spreading his magnificent white wings like a mountain eagle, shouted: 'Every comb a red badge of revolt — long live freedom!' And they set upon the officials, pecking at their noses, snapping at their lips and eyes. Shocked and frightened, the delegation dispersed amid a cloud of feathers.

Our audience, electrified, responded with thunderous applause. And as the curtain came down, we, the young actors — and doubtless many members of the whole assembly — were struck by the ingenuity of Sholem Aleichem's tale. In spotlighting an irrational tradition, he had exposed the cruel logic that could flow like a dark undercurrent beneath the lofty human impulse to redemption.

☙ Bible and Bund ☙

Jewish Antiquity, virtually the code-name in our school for *Tanach*, was taught by Falk Melman, a bald, bespectacled, unassuming gentleman, an astute scholar of incredible patience and a tendency to be manipulated by his students — all of which had earned him the unkind epithet 'Shmelke'.

Nearly seventy years have passed since I sat in his class, yet I haven't forgotten how deftly Melman banished religiosity from the Bible. How skilfully he proved that the *Tanach*, the narrative of the Jewish people, is essentially a piece of secular literature, forced by Orthodoxy into the straitjacket of religion. How carefully he explained that, despite our school's socialistic ideals, it was not Marx's economics but the visions of our biblical prophets which were at the heart of humanity's universal dream.

The *Tanach*, said Melman, was a compilation of folktales, parables, myths and history. Often harmoniously contradictory, it contained the whole world of antiquity, and its position at the centre of all great literature and ethics was indisputable. On one occasion, to reinforce his argument he began to read a short tale by a poet unknown to us.

'I am hostage to a dream,' it began, 'a dream of a galaxy of words orbiting a book on fire which the flames cannot consume. The orbit is divided into three separate spheres: the first ring, closest to the flames, beams with effulgence. The second, further away, twinkles with little sparks of light. The third, remote, lies in darkness. I notice how, at the ring of effulgence, men are walking in and out. One of them, a laughing tear in his eye, is a certain Sholem Aleichem, fiddler of Anatevka. He is speaking with a younger, aristocratic figure, who wears a black cape, walks with a cane, and is called Peretz, progenitor of Bontsha the Silent. "You know," says the old man, pointing his finger at the burning book, "if not for its flames, men would spend their whole lives in darkness." The other looks at him uncertainly. "But reading the flames the wrong way," adds the fiddler, "causes blindness."'

❧ *Zev the Storyteller* ❧

We met on the eve of the great vortex — I, the teenage scribbler, and he, the published storyteller in his mid-thirties. I had plucked up my courage and given him a story of mine to read; a few weeks later, to my astonishment, he asked me to his home for a cup of coffee — an accolade seldom bestowed by a famed writer on a boy like me, for it was a time when a penman was equal to a prince, especially in a land where nearly a quarter of the populace could not read or write.

Zev was a tall, imposing man, neatly dressed, with an Adam's apple that protruded restlessly from his thin throat. He wore a pince-nez on his sharp nose, and had the air of one forever surprised by everything that took place in the world.

'Well, young man,' he began in a sing-song voice, after taking a sonorous sip of his hot coffee. 'Language does not give birth to a story; a story must give birth to language.'

Deaf to what was probably a tactful opening for the criticism of my effort that would follow, I barged in excitedly. 'Is it not a little like mathematics?' I offered. 'Most people are familiar with the numbers of our, so to speak, mathematical alphabet, yet very few of them are mathematicians.'

'Not entirely,' he nodded, 'though you're not far off the mark. In my opinion, a good storyteller must be at home with his people's folklore, their legends, lullabies, their superstitions. And more than anything, he has to know from whence he came, and to where he is going. Without these fundamentals, he might compose very nice, even clever tales, but they will be as enduring as an epitaph written with one finger on the surface of a lake. Let me tell you a little story from chassidic literature.

'A youth came to see the sage known as the Baal Shem Tov — a mystic who could discern a ray of sun in the darkness of night, who could detect the Messiah's footfall at the beginning of time, who proclaimed that the mind which dwells in one's heart creates a better man than that which reigns over one's head. "Master," pleaded the boy, "I have a great need to pray to God, yet I cannot read the prayer-book. My parents were poor, and there was no money for schooling."

'The Baal Shem Tov smiled warmly at the boy. "You cannot read, but perhaps you know the letters of the alphabet?"

'"Yes, that much I do know, sir."

'"Good. Then listen, my young friend. Open up your soul while zealously reciting those letters of the alphabet, from beginning to end, and I promise you that the Almighty Himself will compose for you a psalm which cannot be found in any prayer-book."'

At this point, Zev stopped and drew another loud sip of his now cold coffee, before continuing. 'A good writer,' he said, 'carries his ideas like precious birds in his heart's cage. His tale is the sky of their freedom.'

He paused, and stooped down until his eyes were level with mine.

'And remember — the writer may not be the one who announces to himself, *I am about to write a story.* He is the one to whom, during a sleepless night or in the midst of the busiest day, the story rises up and demands: *Write me!*'

❧ Yiddish Rhapsody ❧

As a girl you were already a young maiden, ripening into motherhood. To your starving children you unbuttoned your generous bodice and opened your heart, that they might receive nourishment and sustenance from your spirit.

And yes, you loved them, mother-bride. And your child-poets, their jealous wives by their sides, lay with you.

Ah, how quickly you matured into a song of love, of peace, of ironic wit. You became the dread of the mighty, and little wonder. They knew well your music's rallying power — you were a stubborn flag standing tall and fluttering against the unjust winds.

Even when shadows grew long and the world became a den of thieves, forcing your children out into the night, you remained in their midst — you were a beacon of light for as long as the dark prevailed.

When the sun rose anew and the remnants slowly returned to their homes, you still walked among them singing psalms of grace. In time they settled their meagre belongings and found comfort — and they shut their doors in your face.

I knew of a poet who dreamt he had walked behind your hearse. Later, as the coffin, still open, was lowered into the pit, he was heard to mutter:

'We will pay a terrible price for this...'

❧ Readers ❧

I belonged to a family of readers. We were all members of the well-known Bronisław Grosser Library, on 68 Zachodnia Street. I would go there two or three times a week, even if I didn't need to borrow or return a book; I just loved the ambience, the company of books, the soothing voices of the librarians, the readers moving about reverently on tiptoe. I always found a corner, and would sit there with my face hidden behind an old newspaper, pretending to read but actually engrossed in thoughts about fantastical realities and the lucidity of the great masters who gazed down upon me questioningly from the brown shelves brimming with books.

On one occasion I had the good fortune, due to the scarcity of space around the little tables, to sit and overhear a hushed conversation between two well-read men, perhaps scholars, one as thin as a reed with a voice as soft as a mouse's whisper, the other on the corpulent side and rather huskily spoken.

'Sense and simplicity are the most essential thing about writing,' the thin one remarked. 'As Chekhov said, one should write so that no reader needs any explanation from the author.'

'Yes, but we cannot reject intricacy and ambiguity out of hand,' his husky companion replied. This was more to my liking.

'Of course we can't. The way I see it, however, a book written with simple clarity exemplifies a greater virtue, and therefore makes a more valuable contribution to the restoration of the human spirit—'

'Speaking of restoration,' the other man interrupted, 'I just purchased, from an antiquarian dealer, a book of short stories published in the late eighteenth century. Its title-page is torn out, so I don't know who the author was. One of the stories concerns a Christian mission somewhere in the north of South America. Several of its members encounter, in the Amazon jungle, a hungry, injured savage who has never heard of God. They take him in, feed him, and, after restoring his health, teach him civility and the Bible and instruct him in the ways of their God. But one night, as the moonlight spears the savage's face, he awakens and without a word sets about slaying all the people within reach, screaming: "A curse on you for giving me this god!"'

'Wait a minute!' the thin scholar exclaimed. 'Isn't that just a version of the Caliban myth?'

'I doubt it. Shakespeare's message is all about language, not God. Anyway, my friend, we need to allow for a certain ambiguity on the part of the master, wouldn't you say?…'

Back home at dinnertime I sat in a daze, my head spinning, for I had understood only half of what the scholars had been debating. But when mother placed an extra slice of meat on each of our plates, I came to, and quickly realized that something festive was afoot. 'What's going on?' I asked.

'We are honouring our new acquisition,' father announced, and he produced the object in question — a hefty book with solid green covers and lettering embossed in gold. It was the Yiddish translation of Ignazio Silone's *Fascism*.

After reading out the introduction, father slid the volume into place on the improvised shelf of our modest library and, turning to me, said something I shall remember to the end of my days: 'A slave to books,' he said, 'is a free man.'

❧ Comrade Tsap ❧

Director of the well-known Scheibler & Groman textile factory and a prominent Communist in our town, Heinrich Tsap was a generous and likeable man. Tall, broad-shouldered, clean-shaven always, and dressed in a grey suit, white shirt and dark-grey tie, there was something summery about him, a lightness even in winter. His wife Friedl, a slender brunette, wore a white silk blouse, with a string of pearls around her swanlike neck. Their intelligent sixteen-year-old daughter Gretchen, with whom I often played, was like a thin green twig a head taller than I, and to my great disappointment had no breasts.

Tsap wrote a column for one of the leading papers, in which he depicted Hitler as a silly huckster of evil. He was twenty years younger than my parents yet did everything possible to keep the friendship alive, not just out of fondness for my father, with whom he liked to sharpen his wits, but because he was in love with his own secretary Sarah, daughter of a neighbour of ours known as White Haskel. Sarah was a young woman who, in my opinion, would have been any man's nuptial Eden. This girl adored my mother and entrusted her with many intimate secrets. Once, I 'accidentally' overheard Sarah confide that Tsap had asked her to elope with him to the east, his Land of Hope.

Those were stormy times, and, as it turned out, a preamble to the great catastrophe. Father was quite weary of his restless young friend, who was guilty of ideological promiscuity. Tsap had been an ardent Socialist, an Anarchist, a Syndicalist, and was now a Communist. Perhaps this turbulent searcher was privately jealous of father's unshakeable evolutionist beliefs.

In his discussions with my sedate dad, the exuberant Heinrich engaged the whole corpus of highbrow proletarian sloganeering. Father, in his turn, maintained that one should tirelessly seek the simple word, so that one's message could come across dressed in sobriety and common sense. His composure incensed the young debater.

'Oh, you and your common sense!' Tsap fired back on one occasion. 'What has your buddy Léon Blum achieved with *his* non-interventionist common sense?' (This was soon after the defeat of the Spanish Republic.) 'The problem with evolutionary socialism,' he went on, 'is that it is perpetually seeking an alliance with the ruling powers, thereby delivering the starving masses directly into the hands of their tormentors!'

'Your argument,' responded my ever-secure father, 'is a mythical red balloon, without a shred of historical evidence.'

At this moment the voluptuous redhead Sarah walked in. Naked, I reflected, she could easily have replaced Renoir's blonde bather! Not surprisingly, her entrance immediately changed Heinrich's mood. Impaling her with his gaze, he continued as if speaking only to her. 'The Jewish intellectual bourgeoisie,' he said, quite softly now, 'laughed when the huckster equated them with vermin.'

'Well, what do you expect?' father replied. 'The nincompoop calls Sigmund Freud a louse.'

'Oh no, my friend, that's not a matter to be treated lightly.' This time Tsap addressed father directly, his voice betraying emotion. 'One should never forget Raskolnikov, who, in order to justify murder, managed in his mind to turn a fellow human into an insect.'

In August 1939, as the Land of Hope went into partnership with the huckster, Heinrich Tsap paid us his last visit. I remember how fervently he tried to explain to my father the wisdom of Bolshevik dialectic.

Ten days later, the huckster's agents awoke Tsap at midnight, invited his Friedl and Gretchen to take a spin in their black limousine, and directed Heinrich to join them for a little chat in Radogosz, on the outskirts of our city — where, in the silence of a new dawn, the partners of the land of his dreams relieved Comrade Tsap's body of his gentle, tormented head.

∽ The Social Worker ∽

On the subject of the abovementioned White Haskel, father once told us something of this man's history, and of the circumstances surrounding his first dealings with him.

When, about eight years before I was born, my parents moved into the four-storey apartment block where they would live for thirty-odd years, White Haskel — so called because he had the look of a man soaked in detergent — had already established himself not only as a 'social worker', but as a respected beadle of the local synagogue.

Haskel always wore lacquered shoes with rubber soles, black trousers with white pinstripes, and a grey coat of English tweed trimmed with velvet; to look the part, he carried a satchel of soft black leather under his arm. He was married to a small, constantly smiling woman — so constantly that her smile might have been affixed as to a billboard. She bore him four decent sons and three beautiful daughters. Needless to say, he was very much admired in our community.

Yet this man, who paraded about the place as a social worker and beadle of a synagogue, was a thief. Not an ordinary thief, mind you — to call him that would be less than precise, because Haskel never stole anything. For that, he had a well-organized team of young pickpockets. He was merely their guru, so to speak, their strategist, who deftly directed operations from a distance.

Like most prestigious thieves in the city of the waterless river, Haskel was in partnership with our very capable police — mainly with the higher ranks, of course. Consequently his gang worked under a fairly secure umbrella. And since their boss, who would not tolerate incompetence, assured them philosophically that from the beginning of time the smart had always capitalized on the stupid, they were not only never troubled by guilt but, on the contrary, were imbued with a sense of professional pride.

One evening, about a week after my future parents had moved into their new one-room flat, father heard a soft knock on the door, a knock as gentle as the thud of a falling snowflake. Before he had time to say 'Please enter', Haskel, a ginger smile on his ruddy face, had crossed the threshold. After they exchanged the customary neighbourly niceties, mother asked the guest if he would take some tea, for which Haskel was warmly grateful. As soon as he 'discovered' that father was a weaver, Haskel introduced himself as a prominent social worker in town.

A day or so later, the snowflake thud repeated itself on our door and Haskel, his fingers curled around a miniature glass vase, entered the room. 'You know,' he said to father, placing the little offering in my mother's hesitating hands, 'textiles are very much in demand these days. People are starved for a good metre of cloth.' He looked around. 'How about setting up a small factory in your room, it's practically empty anyway. Let's buy a pair of textile machines,' he went on enthusiastically. 'We'll make a mint. I have some spare cash, and I'm sure you must have a bit put aside, so how about it?' And without waiting for an answer, Haskel deposited a fat bundle of notes on the table.

Father was stunned. 'But why? You hardly know me. And how can I ever match an amount like that?'

'My dear partner, you forget that I'm a social worker,' Haskel replied, 'and a social worker must have a good nose for people. If you can't match my contribution, chip in as much as you can scrape together. The rest you can settle later, to the tune of our singing machines!'

Next morning father left early for the nearby town of Zgierz, where he hoped to purchase the textile machines. The journey was quite pleasant, though it was a drizzly day and the tram was packed with happy young people, predominantly men. As he was about to disembark, he found himself abruptly squeezed and jostled, and virtually carried to the footpath — where to his horror he quickly noticed the razor-cut in his breast pocket.

When father returned home, an impatient, radiant-faced Haskel was already awaiting him. '*Nu*, partner, *nu*? How did it go?' Instead of answering, father showed him the slit in his pocket. 'Well,' said Haskel, looking disappointed. 'I may or may not believe you, but I must have my money.'

Father nodded despondently. 'I understand,' he said, 'but I haven't got it at the moment. You'll have to give me some time.'

'Of course, of course,' Haskel rushed to reassure him. 'And trust me, I do feel for you — though I'm afraid the going rate of ten percent will have to apply.' Father did not respond. 'You see, dear neighbour,' the social worker went on, more sternly, 'in order not to be ruined in the field of communal activities, one must be forever mindful of one's priorities.'

❧ *The Dream of a Fool* ❧

Berl Sokol, our local electrician, was a known fool. Why? Because, although he was seldom unemployed, not only was he rarely paid for his labours but, in many instances, he would leave a coin or two on the table of a family in strife — while his wife Dvora sat at home, her arms folded, gazing aimlessly at the vacant ceiling. Yet come evening, without fail she would greet her husband with the same words every time: 'And how is my beautiful fool today?'

The wise contributed little to the wellbeing of mankind, Berl would explain to his wife, adding that they often just caused trouble. 'Look,' he said, with some passion, spreading his strong arms. 'There is none wiser than God, and see what *He* has done! Personally, I pray for the Messiah's *non*-coming, because they say his arrival will bring an end to foolishness, and God knows what sort of world such a professional, self-appointed sage would create for us!'

Needless to say, Berl the fool was our local atheists' delight, especially when he mocked what he called the 'empty rabbinical ceremony of words', and the way the rabbis had always dismissed out of hand, indeed ridiculed, the importance of the fool in the cosmic scheme.

'Last Sabbath,' Berl remarked to his companions on one occasion, 'I heard the learned leader of our congregation telling his worshippers the story of Sodom — of how Lot's wife looked back and was thereupon turned into a pillar of salt. "No, no!" I shouted at the top of my voice. "That wasn't her sin. Her sin was that she was longing for the evil she was leaving behind, and for those who knew how to do evil!" The rabbi, incensed, screamed back at me: "I'll have you excommunicated, you silly dreamer!" I smiled at him. "Where dreams end," I retorted, quietly but firmly, "there wickedness begins."'

That night, Berl had had a vision of the rabbi, cane in hand, chasing him from the town. He told his wife about the dream. 'I took to the road in search of a new place,' he explained. 'I walked through winter and summer, crossed many forests, fields and rivers, until finally I reached the famous town of Chelm...'

'And where was *I*?' his beloved cut in.

'Ah, you're too smart to be in a dream like that, sweetheart!... Anyway, there I was, at the iron gates of the town, it was just before dinnertime. I banged my fist against the rusty metal, and immediately heard a voice. *Who are you, stranger*, said the voice, *and what do you want?* "I am Berl the fool," I replied, "and I'm looking for a place to rest my head, for I am weary of the world of sages." *Entry can be granted only on the following condition*, said the voice. *You must answer three questions. If you are a true fool, you will not have any problems. Here are the questions:*

'*What is a life at birth? What is a life at maturity? What is a life at death?*

'I answered at once. "Sir," I called back, "a life at birth is an enigma; at maturity it is an impostor; and at death, a fool!"

'No sooner had I uttered the word *fool* than the gates swung apart and, accompanied by a fanfare from a row of golden trumpets, I was escorted to the king himself. "I've heard you're quite a fellow, Berl," said the king. "Thank you, sir," I replied. He waved his hand to silence me. "...But you cannot stay here for ever. There is a time limit. You see, our own fools are quite xenophobic, I'm afraid, especially seeing as you came here without a permit."

'Well, you can imagine my surprise. I was about to protest but he raised his hand again. "When you leave us," said his royal highness, "please take a message to the outside world." And for the first time he smiled, almost foolishly, before continuing. "Wise men are incomplete," he said at last. "They lack that which makes us fools — envy and hope."'

⇜ *Natasha's Fire* ⇝

Another of the many backyard stories that shaped our micro-cosm concerned Rachmiel, alias Romain, orphaned at the age of two when both his parents died in a fire. He was brought up by his wise but strictly religious grandfather, Aron the tailor. After Rachmiel graduated from primary school, his grand-father said, 'Enough. A trade is better than book-learning. There is just as much wisdom in a swift needle with a whisper-ing yarn in its ear. Remember, son,' he urged, 'a needle behind the lapel and a thimble in the pocket are a passport to the whole wide world.'

But Rachmiel had no head for tailoring; his head was in books, journals, papers, and yet more books. In fact, it was his infatuation with the novel *Jean-Christophe* by Romain Rolland which prompted him to adopt his cherished writer's name. Yet his devoted grandfather wouldn't give up — he knew what lay in store for a man without trade, family or money. And so, after many trials and tribulations, many verbal and at times even physical admonitions, young Romain somehow managed to make the grade, not as a fully-fledged tailor but as a mender.

Come autumn, when the rainy winds had laid Aron low with a peculiar cough, the old man called his grandson to his bedside. 'Rachmiel,' he said, 'you're my only heir. Once I go, the workroom and all its treasures — shoulder-pads, linings, canvas, rolls of cotton, needles and thimbles — all of it will be yours. I am giving you bread and a knife: take it, son, take it and use it wisely.'

Seven days after Aron went the way of all flesh, the young man reverently took down his grandfather's sign, EXPERT TAILOR, and replaced it with his own more modest MENDER. To his surprise he did quite well: within a short time he had become known as the Mender of Bałuty. And as it happened, the daughter of his neighbour Yosl the cobbler was walking God's earth with a soul that was in dire need of mending.

Nacha had a white face as pure as virgin snow, but the glitter in her big black eyes could set any man on fire. Like many young girls of her time, she longed for education, knowledge, and love. And there, right across the yard, was Romain. Although his grandfather's religious teachings never really left him, Romain already belonged to a revolutionary party of free-thinkers. This made him a more than desirable mentor to Nacha — who, free spirit that she was, overnight became Natasha. Each day after work, Romain taught her the history of the October Revolution, and also the art of dialectic and debate which he had acquired among his political comrades. The best way to defeat an opponent, he would tell Natasha, was to make him think. The girl was swept off her feet, and after a few short lessons became a permanent pupil in Romain's academy. At day's end, as the fiery sun set the horizon aflame, Romain would draw the curtains, cradle her to him, and croon into her eager ear a song popular with our street singers:

Natasha, oh my dark Natasha
Kiss my hair, my burning lips...

Then they would breathlessly shed their clothes and entwine themselves in each other's passion. The neighbourhood looked askance on this unholy union, but could do nothing about it. 'I don't need a rabbi's blessing,' Natasha would declare, 'to sleep with my beloved.'

The winter of 1928 was a bitterly cold one. Mountains of insurmountable snow lay everywhere — in the mornings, people inhabiting ground-floor dwellings had to jump out through their windows, since the snow was up to their door-handles. As daylight began to dim and evening shadows climbed our walls, a white frost with a thousand weird and fearful images would invade the windowpanes. It grew murderously cold; to make matters worse, the coalminers went on strike.

One Friday morning Natasha awoke earlier than usual. She decided to light the stove before Romain began his day's work. All at once — no one will ever know how — the whole room was engulfed in flames.

Ousted from their paradise, the two lovers — barefooted and clad only in their underwear — stood shivering in the snow-white yard, surrounded by their bewildered neighbours. Everyone was convinced that the fire was punishment for their ungodly behaviour. Later, over a plate of hot porridge, Yosl the cobbler, who had divorced his wife for promiscuity soon after their daughter Nacha's birth, pleaded with the couple to mend their ways, as heaven was clearly against them. Romain remained silent. How could he convince Yosl that he had divorced heaven for the same reason the cobbler had divorced his wife?

'Well, Reb Yosl,' the young man said at last, 'you know the old saying: *meshane mokom, meshane mazal* — a change of place, a change of luck…'

A dismayed Yosl accompanied them to where the gutter separated the cobblestone yard from the pavement. He watched with a pang in his heart as the couple walked slowly away. He was still standing there long after Nacha had disappeared beyond his homely horizon forever.

❧ *Nemesis* ❧

Reb Nachman the kosher slaughterer, his wife Chana and their buxom eighteen-year-old daughter Reizl occupied the ground-floor apartment of our tenement. Reizl's face was an open letter of adoration — indeed, her beauty had no equal in the neighbourhood. She worked at home as an embroiderer, and since this work demanded good light, Reb Nachman placed her machine at the window, so that the sill became an extension of her working space.

How was Reb Nachman to know that this would put his daughter face to face with a young joiner, the intense union leader Motl, known as Hercules, who shortly afterwards established his own workplace in a neighbouring flat, in a window directly opposite Reizl's? How could Nachman know that it was his daughter who, not unwittingly, ignited the flame of desire in Motl's heart? Or that one fateful evening, Motl dropped a red rose on Reizl's windowsill?

But Nachman's wife Chana knew. She knew how Reizl secretly took the rose to her bed; how she softly invoked Motl's name in the night, whispering that he was the reason for her existence, murmuring words of eternal bliss while her fingers sought out her private parts.

Chana was not sure how to bring all this to her husband, but she was certain that such a sickness required immediate attention. The moment Nachman finished his morning prayers, she plucked up her courage and, with tears in her eyes, reminded him of all the potential perils that lay in wait for their unmarried daughter. That very afternoon the local matchmaker, Reb Fajvl, paid the family a surprise visit.

'My dear friend,' the matchmaker began, addressing Nachman, 'the rich widower Shlomo Levi, who is just forty, is in dire need of a wife and a mother for his two gorgeous little girls. If you agree to have him as a son-in-law, you could wish each other *Mazel Tov* tomorrow.'

Like a flame, Reizl shot up from her workbench. 'Who sent for you, Reb Fajvl? Who asked you to find a match for me? Please take your proposition elsewhere. I already have a groom — I'll marry him, or no one.'

'Reizl, Reizl,' her mother cried. 'How can you shame your old father like this? Amongst our people, it's the parents' choice as to who marries whom.' The girl made no answer; she bit her lip, sat down at her machine and resumed working.

Before I knew it, I had become the lovers' trusted messenger. I read every word they wrote to each other. I can still recall their last communication exactly. 'Dearest Motl,' she implored, 'please hurry and rescue me from this disaster, or I'll die. Yours forever, Reizl.' 'Sweetheart,' he responded, 'I have just received notice to make myself available at once for military service. We can't run away as we planned, but on my very first leave we can become husband and wife.'

Meanwhile the wedding preparations were in full swing. Chana and Nachman were overjoyed, and understood their daughter's paleness and moody demeanour as the natural signs of a maiden's pre-nuptial anxiety. It is a task beyond the best of pens, therefore, to describe their pain and desolation when, at daybreak on the appointed morning, they found Reizl's bed empty. Their howls mobilized the whole neighbourhood. To do a thing like this to one's parents, people said, a daughter had to have a heart of stone. What they all overlooked, of course, was that the gentler the heart, the heavier the stone.

Three days went by — though to Chana and Nachman they felt like three long years — and there was no trace of Reizl. In desperation, her mother visited a seer. 'Go ten kilometres in a straight line from where you live,' the seer advised, 'then turn right and walk five more. Sit by the lake and wait until the moon comes out. You will hear the song your daughter heard, and you will know.'

Chana went. She found the lake, and sat beside it until the moon emerged. At first she heard nothing. Then, out of the gloom, there arose (she was certain) a distant, beautiful voice:

I am Rusalka, the lake-fairy,
Abandoned alone,
Come to me, Reizl, my sweetheart,
Make my bed your home.

Reizl was buried by the cemetery fence. Although it was raining. there were hundreds of mourners at her funeral. After they had dispersed, I saw a soldier approach the grave. He bent down and planted a red rose in the moist soil. For a long time he just stood there, like a stone statue, ignoring the downpour. When the sky was about to swallow the last morsel of light, he turned and slowly walked away.

❦ *A Deadly Dance* ❦

The landscape of my youth, before the curtain fell, had a certain charm, an aura of the impoverished yet playful; but more than anything else there was an aroma of eccentricity. Ours was primarily a land of schism — of Socialists against Communists, of Anarchists against Legislators, of benevolent societies against crooks and exploiters; a land of great loves and betrayals.

Our good-looking Abrasha was a bit of a vagabond, as well as a trained singer, who made his living in winter by playing cards and in summer by singing in the street. He was also a kind of political chameleon, for he seemed to belong to all parties: on election day for our municipal council you could find him on a different corner every hour, preaching a different ideology. Yet this happy-go-lucky individual was much loved, especially by women, mainly mature ones. Young girls, he would say, were nothing but trouble.

Since he was a singer, he equated everything in life with a song. For example, one of our neighbours, Malkale (who happened to be endowed with a rather impressive bosom), he would describe as a filled-out soprano in dire need of a strong baritone. Every morning, after Malkale's husband Mendl had left for work, Abrasha, who was Mendl's brother, would position himself securely outside her window, crooning:

O Dolores, please don't make a fuss;
Let me love you, no one is watching us.

I'm not sure how long this went on, but one night, at about two o'clock, there was a frantic knocking on our door. My whole family woke in alarm, and when father opened the door Mendl fell sobbing into his arms.

'Mashinka, Mashinka,' he wailed, turning to my mother, Masha. 'It hurts! It hurts from here to here, from here to here!' He repeated this a hundred times, pointing into his chest. 'What am I to do? I caught them in the act, in the very act!... You know,' he continued, as mother handed him a cold drink to quieten him down, 'I asked that bastard brother of mine, *Hey, what do you think you're doing?* And he unashamedly answered, *A tango!* and flew out.'

Mendl fell back in his chair, sweating all over. It was a miracle he didn't suffer a heart attack.

Life in our tenement was full of open secrets. One morning, as Mendl was about to shave his chin, he noticed in the mirror his voluptuous but unreachable wife stepping naked from her bed. This incensed him so much that he hurled a little stool into the looking-glass, and all of a sudden saw himself staring back at himself, fragmented into ghastly triangular shards. Was this the straw that broke Mendl's back? Or was it the fact that he couldn't satisfy his Malkale the way Abrasha did? Hard to say. Obviously he was made wretched by his hatred of a love miscarried, and so this quiet, mild-mannered Mendl became his own monster.

I cannot remember the day of the week, but I can still see the black hearse rolling into our yard, two sombre-looking men sliding the coffin into the vehicle, Malkale's arm hooked firmly into the arm of Mendl's handsome brother, both of them dressed in black, and — under the watchful eyes of our entire tenement block — walking bowed behind the funeral procession.

The following day was like any other, and yet not the same. Abrasha stopped singing and Malkale didn't stop crying; but it was White Haskel, our very own social worker, who voiced his consoling opinion outside their window. 'Suffering in the present,' he was heard to advise the grief-stricken lovers, 'will not expiate the crimes of the past.'

❧ *The Assimilator* ❧

On a bright Sunday morning in June, a friend of my father's, a small insignificant-looking free-thinker known as Pinchas the Logician — whose week was made up of seven Sundays — was sitting at leisure in a local park, trying to work out the reason behind the random motions of the celestial bodies. Presently he spotted a figure making its way towards him, and behold, it was his former neighbour Lev Solewicz, who, because of his disgust with the Yiddish language and the people who spoke it, had moved away from our neighbourhood and transformed himself into Leon Solarski.

'Well, well,' said Leon in his newly adopted tongue, 'what a refreshing pleasure to see a man who, like myself, has had the courage to reject religious claptrap, long beards, sidelocks, fur hats, and all that.'

'Quite so, my dear friend,' the Logician replied. 'And yet I still remain the authentic Jew I have always been.'

'Really? How's that?'

'By the very fact that I cry whenever I hear that a Jew like you has been beaten up.'

'But I am *not* a Jew, not any more,' Leon shot back, indignant. 'And what's more, I'll soon be converting!'

'Have a seat, Lev,' said Pinchas in his politest Yiddish, 'and let me tell you a story.'

At this Leon flared up. 'Don't you dare call me *Lev*,' he cried. 'And don't speak to me in your corrupted half-German!'

'Whoa, hold it, hold it…' The Logician raised his palms, as if offering a truce. 'Rage is a fool's trade and I don't think you qualify — not yet.' He smiled and continued quietly: 'So please, join me on this bench and let me tell you a little story. You may find it quite… enlightening.'

Leon sat down reluctantly, checked his watch, and turned to Pinchas with a look of mock-resignation.

'I knew a man,' the Logician began, 'who forsook his father's wisdom, his mother's warmth, the fount of hope which had nourished their dreams by candlelight, and he exchanged his parents' ancient truths for a strange new god. Like Adam he stood in a hostile land, stuttering in his new tongue, with hands outstretched, a beggar awaiting a scrap of mercy. He died alone. Nobody walked behind his hearse — except the stone-mason, whom he had instructed to inscribe above his tomb an epitaph that would sum up a wasted existence. It read:

> *A cat dreamt he was a tiger*
> *And dreaming, lost his wits.*
> *He fell asleep in the arms of a tiger*
> *And woke up torn to bits.'*

Lev-Leon shook his head. 'Save your preaching for some-body else,' he said, making no effort to disguise his irritation. 'I've listened to enough sermons in my time. After I'm gone I don't care what my epitaph says. What matters is life, not death.'

As he hurried off, his last words echoed in the Logician's mind like a rifle-shot.

❧ *The Philosopher* ❧

Mechel Schiff, my father's friend, would show up every Sunday morning to tell stories and partake of a hot cooked breakfast. The rest of the week he was fed by the Christian Mission, somewhere on Wólczańska Street. A stocky, red-headed, blue-eyed chap, who dwelt for most of his life in a dilapidated shed, Mechel was known as *Der Hosenkavalier* because, as he himself put it, 'I come from a line of fastidious dressers'. At the start of spring, this unemployed philosopher would visit the local market, where for one złoty he would purchase an entire new wardrobe. He would spend 20 groschen on a pair of shoes, 10 on a shirt, 25 on a jacket, and another 5 on socks and a tie; the balance, a whole 40 groschen, he always chose to invest in a pair of *hosen* — trousers, according to him, being the most important item in a man's wardrobe. Then, Mechel, the highly intelligent atheist, was off to the Christian Mission for a free meal.

'And how was the soup today, Herr Mechel?' enquired the head of the Mission, Johann Mentzeler, who had been trying for years to convert Mechel to the right path.

'Fabulous,' Mechel retorted. 'I imagine that is the way they cook in your paradise kitchen, Herr Johann.'

'That's true, that's true,' Johann jumped up, excited. 'I'm glad you can finally see a glimpse of the true light.'

'Sir, I said it merely by way of conversation. But to be quite honest, I must confess– '

'Yes, that's it!' Johann almost shrieked with joy. 'Confess! Confess!'

'—that I am more absorbed,' Mechel continued, ignoring the intrusion, 'with the economics of *this* world, than with the culinary art of the next. And to be truthful, I must lodge a small complaint: some mischievous devil, I know not of which denomination, has pinched the traditional marrowbone out of my soup.'

'Yes, so I see,' Johann replied, blushing. 'But surely, in order to be happy, one must learn to detach oneself from such trivialities.'

'Sir — a marrowbone is not a triviality. Not just to me, but even to the most stoutly religious believer.'

Johann was not to be outdone. 'Ah, well, Herr Mechel. I know that some of your people are such stout believers that they fast every Monday and Thursday.'

'True, Herr Johann. But that is not an expression of their belief — rather of the lack of it.'

'Ah, Herr Mechel, dear Mechel, you are so clever! If only you could learn to love God — to understand God — to come to Him…'

'Of course I can, and I will — but not until such time as a fellow can be locked up behind bars for preaching religion. So that no devil will ever dare to help himself to the marrowbone in my soup, which in their wisdom the gods — whatever their persuasion — have bestowed upon their beloved Mechel Schiff.'

≈ *Yankl Bolshevik* ≈

It was not by proper given-name and surname that a person was officially known in the territory of our community, but by his or her acquired nickname. For instance, if you were to state that Mr Samuel Haberman had passed away, no one would know to whom you were referring; but should you remark that lame Shmuel had kicked the bucket, a shudder-sigh of recognition and grief would run like an evening whisper through the minds of our tender-hearted citizens.

Yankl Zelmanowicz, father of my school friend Laibush, and the man who had taught us to play Five Hundred (not that I needed any coaching), was known as Yankl Bolshevik. I am not sure that he was ever a true Communist; rather, from his political jargon I would conjecture that he was a member of the legendary SR, the Social Revolutionaries, a party that sometimes resorted to terror — though one should not equate that with the random banditry of more recent times. If, for example, the committee decided to take out a man for murdering his comrades, it had to be that particular individual alone; should the potential victim have even a dog beside him, the assassination would not take place.

Our Yankl had an analytical mind, and he loved to measure everything against his beloved Russian Revolution. 'You know, children,' he told us once, watching his son Laibush shuffle a worn-out deck of cards, 'I often recall those monumental October days. History dealt the Russian people a terrific hand, yet some of our major players — like Zinoviev, Kamenev, even the great Victor Chernov, leader of the SR, a man I loved like a father — all of them pulled back at the crucial moment. It needed the ingenuity of an Ilyich Lenin, who took one look and declared: "Comrades, Red is our winning colour. Let's play!"'

Yankl Bolshevik was soaked in fascinating stories — stories of night battles in snowstorms against White armies led by the bloodthirsty Denikin, Kolchak and others. But to me, the most unforgettable of all was the story of Maria Spiridonova's return from Siberia; when he spoke about her, his eyes were aflame with black fire. Perhaps there was something more between him and the legendary great lady of the Social Revolutionaries!

'I was amongst a thousand men or more,' he would begin, 'who awaited her on the outskirts of Moscow. As the train, its face draped with two red banners, came into view, we ran towards the driver, asked him to unhook the engine, and joyously harnessed *ourselves* to her carriage. Beholding that spectacle, Maria, this humble heroine, jumped from the train to haul our load with us; then, at the top of her lungs, she sang out the great opening words of the *Internationale*:

> *Arise ye workers from your slumbers*
> *Arise ye prisoners of want…*

and, like a mighty peal of thunder, a thousand voices responded as one:

> *So comrades, come rally*
> *And the last fight let us face;*
> *The Internationale*
> *Unites the human race.'*

Yankl would spend his Saturday mornings at the barber's. Here, Jews who could hardly make ends meet argued richly and passionately about Sacco and Vanzetti, Hitler, Spain, Mussolini and the war in Abyssinia, the famine in China, and a hundred other topics. A barbershop in those days was a political marketplace, and Yankl was always in the thick of the debate.

Although, in the wake of the Moscow trials, Yankl became a disillusioned man, come May Day he would still stand in front of the barber's — dressed in a black dinner-suit with a red flower in his lapel — and as the procession passed by, he, the old Bolshevik, would shine once more. I saw him taking the 'salute' during our last May Day parade. He already knew that Russia's revolutionary spirit had been imprisoned in Stalin's gulag, that the children of Ferdinand Lassalle were wearing swastikas, that

Europe was tensed for imminent war. Yet as the *Internationale* burst forth from the throats of ten thousand marchers, his face lit up again with that incredible romantic light. A light that, soon enough, would be extinguished forever.

➳ *Sport* ➳

Imbued with the spirit of the forthcoming Berlin Olympics, some of our fellow citizens embarked on a new yet generations-old sport: pogroms. The old cry went up: *The Jews!* — no one really knew why. But things seldom appear to people the way they really are, only the way they want them to be, and suddenly the land of my birth began to mushroom with pogroms — many, many pogroms. I will relate only the one I witnessed myself.

A mob of university students, in league with some individuals who were intellectually inept, rushed into the house at Zawiszy 7, home of my school friend Zisza Kliger, who dwelt there in a windowless flat with his younger brother and widowed mother. The soberly irrational Olympians ripped apart the only bedding the Kligers possessed, let the feathers fly all over the street like petals of snow, threw the mother's ever-hungry cooking-pots out the window, and knocked her unconscious into the bargain for trying to protect us.

Warming to their task, they made for the home of my friend Huna Kurbic, who lived next door to the Kligers. Huna's father was a gardener, and the only Jew in the city of the waterless river employed in the public service; he was also an old revolutionary who had fought against the Tsars for the independence of our country, and although hardly in his prime, he would not have let these rascals as much as spit in his porridge. But they quickly overpowered him and gave him a good thrashing, and for his temerity he was sacked from his job — for planting (as a bitter jest had it) Jewish trees in Slavic soil.

Encouraged by their successes and by the quiet acquiescence of the authorities, and filled with zest to emulate their Berlin contemporaries, our local heroes soon renewed their crusade; they reappeared on the corner of Zgierska and Limanowskiego, where they caught the seventy-year-old Alter 'Herring' (so called because he dealt in that variety of fish). Two medical students who were part of the gang gave him a proper physical, and to crown their victory they tipped Alter's barrel of herrings into the gutter.

These outbursts and other similar demented deeds and disturbances stirred our town's two organized trade unions into action. Jewish workers, together with an admixture of other men of goodwill, decided to make a stand. The next 'sports event' was scheduled for Sunday, right after the morning church service. The racial athletes gathered under their party flag on the local marketplace, Bałucki Rynek, fervently intoning their saintly hymn:

> To our last drop of blood
> We'll defend our People's right
> Till we rid our sacred land
> Of the ugly Hebrew blight.
> Every Jew is a deadly foe
> So help us God,
> So help us God.

The name of the Almighty was invoked in profound solemnity, with eyes closed.

Haughtily, and in crisp military step, they entered Limanowskiego, my street. But to their bewilderment, they found themselves met by a wall of sternly resolute men armed with iron bars. For a moment they stood there as if paralysed. And then, hoodlums being by their very nature cowards, they took off in all directions, dispersing like a cloud of dust driven off by a gust of wind.

However — as I would learn later, much later — this dust never actually disappeared. It found shelter and settled, to re-emerge all too soon from out of the dark crevices of time.

≈ *The Improviser* ≈

My little friend, pimple-faced Shmulik, lived with his parents and three siblings in an attic no bigger than an alcove. Shmulik was a born improviser. You'd say a word and he'd come back at once with a rhyme. On top of that, Shmulik had the voice of an angel. He could soften a stone with his singing. The young cantor of our local synagogue believed that we had Shmulik's voice to thank for all the mercies the Almighty bestowed upon us.

But our landlord Motke was of another mind. We kids, he said, were the natural enemies of property, and Shmulik, our ringleader, was the worst of all. Perhaps he was right. Anything on his property that could serve the needs of us kids was fair game. Especially Motke's timber yard, just inside the gateway to our block of apartments.

We were twelve youngsters, seven boys and five girls, between the ages of ten and fourteen. We had our own football team and card club, and the timber yard was our logical hideout. It was there that we played cowboys and indians, fathers and mothers, hide-and-seek; above all, we played cards — for real money.

One day Shmulik, the boy with a thousand pimples on his forehead and the voice of an angel, whose plain-looking thirty-year-old sister would shiver while I explored the topography of her meagre body, suggested that in order to stage an authentic adventure of the Wild West, it was necessary to light a fire. Well, there was no shortage of firewood in the timber yard; but the moment the smell of smoke seeped into Motke's flat, he came running, waving his arms, brandishing his black-lacquered cane. 'I'll send you all to prison, you good-for-nothings!' he screamed. 'Prison, you hear? — that's what I'll do!'

Shmulik the improviser stood his ground. 'Prison? Prison?' he repeated, like a fiddler tuning his violin. 'Then allow me, sir,' he announced, effecting a deep bow before the furious Motke. And with one eye closed, tapping his right foot, he began:

From prison to sunny Spain
Shmulik flew in an aeroplane;
I was king of the sea,
No lord was greater than me.

Girls eighteen to the dozen I've had,
Come, pretty maiden, be my bride,
You'll find me talented, and besides
I'm such a well-to-do lad.

On the word 'lad', Shmulik made another deep bow, took off his hat and held it out. Motke shook his head. 'Don't you ever dare to enter my timber yard again,' he hissed, then tossed a small coin into the hat and walked off.

But nothing could discourage our Shmulik. Since we had lost access to our timber citadel, he immediately embarked on a search for a new hideaway. His choice was ingenious: the gently tilted tar roof of our block — where Motke had once kept a pigeon coop, where silence listened to the wind, and where our slightly limping landlord was not game enough to visit. Here we would set up home anew.

We climbed up on the roof by way of the loft (our leader alone had the privilege of arriving directly via his attic window) and we celebrated the occasion with a game of blackjack. Needless to say, Shmulik, may his memory be blessed forever, cleaned us out. Once again he bowed his domed head and, hat in hand, gave his bankrupt admirers another performance:

Shmulik is a clever boy,
He may be in rags but he's never coy;
Don't turn your head, don't even blink
Or he'll take your money in a wink.

I still recall the summery September day in 1942 when Shmulik, escorted by the Jewish police of our inverted state, walked ahead of his family towards the cattle-truck that would take them to be 'resettled'. Shmulik was sad, he looked forlorn — I had never seen him like this. Perhaps he knew intuitively that his career as an entertainer had come to an end.

Years later I had the good fortune to meet up with Shmulik's cantor from the old days, the one who had been so enraptured by his voice. I don't know why people used to say that a cantor is a fool; for as it turned out, this cantor was now a confident, fully accredited rabbi with a long white beard. We were pleased to see one another, but I had barely opened my mouth when he patted me sagely on the shoulder and declared: 'In everything that happened to Shmulik lies God's hand. How else could he have become the head soloist in our heavenly Father's choir? How else?' he repeated, triumphantly.

❦ *Star-crossed Lovers* ❦

The four-storey tenement block where we lived was occupied
by sixteen families. Every family dwelled in a one-room apartment. Each room had two beds: one for the parents, the other
for their four or five children. What better proof of the closeness of our families?

Our landlord Motke — a grey-bearded man who swag-
gered around with a black-lacquered cane and a white handkerchief in his breast pocket; whose quarters comprised *two*
rooms, plus a kitchen, a balcony and a foyer; whose set of gold
front teeth established beyond question his enormous wealth
— this man was known by everyone as Motke Machinist.

Not that he had anything to do with repairing machines.
No. The honorific was bestowed upon him because in his
younger years — that is, before he inhabited a residence with
a foyer — Motke had been one of the most sought-after safe-
breakers. Legend had it that he worked only at night, in his
socks, and with his eyes closed so as not to look upon his
accomplices. Evidently he enjoyed strict solitude.

Motke had a fascinating history. He was a plain-looking,
rather morbid man, yet it had happened that Kraindle — the
most delectable, the smartest, the best-educated prostitute in
the profession, who distributed up front to the needy the
money she made on her back — had fallen passionately in love
with him.

Motke's parents, however, though no more kosher than
he, had refused to have a prostitute, even a noble one, for a
daughter-in-law. Motke protested, threatened to hang himself; Kraindle wept, vowed that she would go straight, swore
that she knew a doctor who could 'make it good as new'. But
Motke's family, especially his mother, would not hear of it.
They soon forced their son to marry the strong-headed Ruchcia,

who by way of a dowry received a fishstall at the market from her father — whom we called Mussolini because he peddled Italian typewriters.

As soon as Kraindle learnt of her defeat she had slit her wrists, and would most probably have bled to death had she not been saved by one of her ever-alert colleagues. Rumour had it that, thanks to her connections in higher circles, she was able to secure a position in the French Foreign Legion...

Meanwhile, every Monday morning Ruchcia would ride in a hired horse-and-buggy to the nearby village, where she bought fish from a young farmer who played the flute. One year, just before the High Holidays, she departed at dusk, never to return.

Mussolini and his wife, Tzerl — who went about moaning, with white compresses pressed to her forehead — ran to the police, hired private detectives, lit candles at the cemetery. But all to no avail. Tzerl's carry-on infected our lives with some bizarre stories. According to one, Ruchcia had been murdered at Kraindle's behest; another had Kraindle climbing through Motke's window at night; a third was put about by a self-proclaimed seer who announced that it was 'definitely a young flautist' he had seen in his dream, whipping with a dead fish the flesh of the hapless Ruchcia, harnessed to his buggy...

Years later (when Motke's parents had long been playing canasta with the angels) — after a plague of grey hornets had assailed our skies, and all the familiar stories had been torn up and tossed into the basket of oblivion; after the difficult times that had descended on our lives, times of cruelty, restriction, confiscation, confinement, and the exodus, finally, of even the mice from our microcosm — Motke was still living in the same tenement block. Without a family, without a friend, he looked an old and broken man, though he was no more than sixty. He had been exiled from his apartment to the attic on the roof, where the beastly cold wind reigned supreme. One day he told himself, 'Enough is enough,' and on the first available occasion added his name to a list of men due to be shipped out from our inverted kingdom.

Accordingly, one wintry frosty noon, Motke climbed into the cattle-truck that would deliver him to another land. Then a strange thing happened, something that no one could ever explain. People swore that they saw Kraindle walking beside him, holding on tight, her still-radiant head resting on his drooped shoulder. 'Kraindle, what has brought you here?' Motke was heard to call out. 'Jealousy,' his escort replied. 'I'll not let Lady Death have you all to herself!'

❧ Interrupted Song ❧

Speaking of Motke, I must back-track for a moment, for Motke always brings to mind the Goldhamers. They were a family of six — father, mother and four children — who had become members of our four-storey tenement community back in 1933, and whom our landlord held in the highest regard because of their sedateness, piety, and dependability as tenants who never failed to pay their rent on time.

Isaac Goldhamer, thanks to his enormous size, was immediately nicknamed '*Byk*' (Ox). A very strictly religious man, Isaac presided over his fruit business dressed in traditional black garb, with a prayer always on his lips. One of his boys, Simcha, was my age; his brother Moniek, though two years younger, was nevertheless equally eligible to be accepted as a fully-fledged member of our backyard football team. As a rule, however, a beating preceded the initiation of anyone who desired to enter our fellowship, and on this occasion I volunteered to carry out the job. After school, in the dark cobble-stone entrance to the yard, I lay quietly in wait for my two victims. Or so I thought. After the thrashing the two brothers gave *me*, my own mother couldn't recognize me!

And yet almost overnight the three of us became close friends. Little Moniek even confided a secret that he kept from his own brother – that he would rather be called 'Moishe Shambelo', and when he grew up he would be leader of an underworld gang, living in caves frequented by a fraternity of robbers. Both brothers had fine voices, especially Simcha, and they consequently became choristers in the Great Synagogue on Wolborska Street (which the Germans, to prove their Aryan superiority, would later burn to the ground).

On Rosh Hashana, the Jewish New Year, Simcha asked me to join him at the morning service. This was an awesome experience, for I had never been inside a synagogue before. So many Jews, all enveloped in the white wings of prayer-shawls! Then there was the singing of the choir – and above all the voice of Simcha, chiming like a brass gong in the cupola of a holy temple.

Avinu malkenu…

That night I confessed to father that I had spent the day in synagogue. 'You did the right thing, son,' he said. I was taken aback: 'But why? We're not religious.' 'The synagogue is a fortress of *Yiddishkeit*,' he explained, 'and we are *Yidn*.' I was still puzzled: 'Aren't we also socialists?' 'Of course, though primarily Yiddish socialists,' he replied. 'How is that?' I persisted. 'Well, did our circumcision not come before our social-ism?' And father closed the inquiry with a smile.

Encouraged by this confusion, I managed to talk all my backyard friends into becoming members of Skif, the Socialist Children's Union. When our Skif choir was preparing itself for a concert in aid of the workers combating Fascism in Austria,

Simcha proved a most welcome recruit, and was duly appointed to sing solo the main theme-song of our production. This arrangement turned out to be a rather traumatic experience. The whole choir was assembled on stage, the curtain was about to go up, but no Simcha! And there was no last-minute arrival, because our star never showed up.

When I got home I discovered that Simcha's father had got wind of the whole affair and had locked up his son for the day in a dark closet. Spotting me in the yard, Isaac Goldhamer burst from his door like an unstoppable bullock. 'If you ever involve my children in your gang of *Apikorsim*,' he shouted, 'I'll skin you alive!'

For years I lost track of Simcha. I caught up with him in November 1944, in the slave-labour camp of Wolfsberg. He was singing to entertain the *kapos* for a slice of bread. Haggard, worn to the bone, he had no life left in him. At roll-call next morning he was selected to be transported to the Auschwitz gas chambers. The deputy commandant, who was known as Henk, asked Simcha if he had heard of the singer Joseph Schmidt. Simcha said that he had. 'And do you know his famous song?' 'Yes, Herr Unterscharführer.' 'So let me hear you.' 'I've forgotten the words, sir.' 'Then let me teach them to you. *This is the final day, of my existence; this is my final day, I can be sure…*' But Simcha, already in the open truck, remained mute. 'Damn Jew,' screamed the officer. 'Damn Jew, *sing*!' My friend's lips stayed firmly sealed. Then, as the truck began to move, Simcha looked straight into Henk's eyes and, with his last ounce of strength, let his voice fly. It resounded once again like the chime of a brass gong:

Avinu malkenu…

Though this time beneath the unblemished blue of an indifferent cosmic cupola.

❧ *The Melamed* ❧

I cannot quite remember how it came about, but one evening, as mother was dishing out our dinner, I heard her say: 'Gershon, I'm about to engage a melamed for our son.' A melamed was a religious teacher. 'I don't think the extra study will interfere with his school program, and it will enhance his knowledge of Jewish history.' Father's non-response was a sign of acquiescence.

But my older sister Pola, a confirmed Marxist who had already done time for the glory of Stalin in a couple of prestigious Polish prisons, would not hear of it. 'Why, mother?' she pleaded. 'Why should you introduce your son, at such a vulnerable age, to that opium?'

Father, a sworn atheist who quarrelled with God all his life, chuckled. He was a socialist but, like many others of his comrades, of the Fabian persuasion. Once, in a discussion, I heard him remark that if Marx had been born into money, he would never have written *Das Kapital*. In fact, father argued, Marx hated the very class he yearned to belong to.

Next day after sundown, as I was finishing my homework, Eliahu the melamed arrived. He was a smallish man with a very sympathetic face, but without one solitary hair on his chin. What's this, I thought, a rabbi without a beard? After he left I asked father — who, at the other end of the table, had pretended to read the paper while listening attentively to my first lesson — how it was that the rabbi's face was as smooth as a baby's bottom. 'Well, son,' he replied, 'better a rabbi without a beard than a beard without a rabbi.'

Father had clearly taken a liking to the man, and so had I. Eliahu began each lesson with a story from the *Chumash* (the Pentateuch, or Five Books of Moses), to which I would listen with a certain juvenile scepticism. Yet these stories opened up a new world. It was not that I hadn't heard them already from my teachers at school; but Reb Eliahu knew how to add fire to these wondrous tales, and they set my boyish head spinning.

One evening, as mother interrupted the simmer of the kettle on the stove and poured hot tea into white enamel cups, the melamed asked my father: 'Reb Gershon, why do you not send your son to a proper religious school where they teach about the Almighty and His *real* glory?'

My father smiled. 'You mean about our personal Creator, the one who governs our lives? Well, Reb Eliahu, the Creator's track record is not a very good one, especially in relation to His chosen.' He said this without a hint of sarcasm.

'Are we to take only the good, without the bad?' the other man retorted.

'Ah, Reb Eliahu, you are talking with Job's tongue. Yet is it not the very book you're quoting which casts the longest shadow on divine justice?'

Eliahu fell silent, his face reddened. He was a refined man, perhaps he felt he had gone too far. Burying his eyes in the steaming cup, he regained his composure. 'You know,' he said, 'there is a school of thought which upholds a theory that the sages consciously placed the Tav, the first letter in the word *Torah*, at the very end of the alphabet — meaning by this to remind us that a man may have a world of knowledge at his fingertips, but without immersing himself in the depths of the Torah he still remains unlearned.'

Father smiled; obviously he loved this fable. For a good while the two men searched one another's eyes. Then my melamed stood up. As father stretched out his hand to him, Reb Eliahu said, 'Thank you, sir,' and with the footfall of a shy child he stepped toward the door and gently closed it behind him.

❦ *The Legend* ❦

On 18 July 1936, Fascist insurgents who would later be led by
General Franco rose up against the legally elected government
of the Spanish Republic. Although Spain was a thousand
kilometres from our town — where unemployment was a way
of life, where little folk were pressed into holes in dilapidated
houses by a system that mocked their misery — the temerity
of the insurgents threw our neighbourhood into a state of
great ferment.

Almost overnight there were demonstrations, meetings,
protests, fundraising drives; people greeted each other with
clenched fists, shouting *Red Front!* And everywhere, our neighbours' son Lucjan was to be found: tall, dark, handsome Lucjan,
reliable Lucjan — alias Luzer, who, forever on the lookout for
answers to the intractable question of the wretchedness in our
midst, had discovered the Soviet Union. Sitting on the shoulders of two comrades, a red flag in his hand, above a tumultuous, ebullient throng that heaved like a stormy sea, Lucjan
sang at the top of his sonorous voice:

> *In smoke sinks Barcelona,*
> *Flames engulf Madrid,*
> *And sailing over Aragon*
> *A golden moon does bleed.*
>
> *Madrid is a tower of light,*
> *In the dark a shining beam;*
> *But Italy sends its bombers*
> *And poison sends Berlin.*

Some two months later, as the papers brought grim news from the front, we heard that Lucjan, in the company of others like himself, tailors who had never held a gun in their hands, was off to join the International Brigade to fight for Spain's freedom. Lucjan's mother cried. 'Please, son, don't do this to your old mother.' His father pleaded. 'Why, Luzer? Why lay down your young life for Spain, what is Spain to you? Have you forgotten what they did to your ancestors, how they murdered us in the tens of thousands, burned us alive in the bonfires?"

But Lucjan was immovable. 'Yes, father, I do remember. But remembering and dwelling on the past are two different things. Dwelling on past tragedies is self-destructive,' said the young party man, 'and I, your son, am going to make sure that Spain never reverts to the those shameful times of the Inquisition.'

On 19 May 1939, as General Franco was taking the salute at his victory parade in Madrid, Lucjan, his right arm in a black sling, limped into our neighbourhood and was greeted by the general acclaim of its inhabitants. His head was bowed in sorrow. It was clear that his inner anguish was far more painful than his physical injuries — the knowledge of defeat, and of the Soviet betrayal.

Two years later we heard him speak, perhaps for the first time since his return; and although we were still teenagers we could tell that the words he wanted evaded him, while those that did come seemed inadequate to express the feelings that filled his heart. But the fact that he had fought in the battles we all dreamt of joining created an extraordinary aura around the young Lucjan, an aura which embraced him like a mantle and lent a special credence to his nickname — for after his return, we rarely referred to him other than as 'The Legend'.

❧ *As the Days Darkened* ❧

No one knew what had come over Szymon, our consumptive mystic-turned-Cassandra. Out of the blue he started running through the city, waving his hands about, shouting: 'People, good people! O hear me, you sinners! Our years will be short-ened by months, our months by weeks, our weeks by days — and all because the mezuzahs on our doorposts are tarnished. The demon is on his way, he is coming, coming! He'll attack out of lust, with great brutality…' And thus screaming, Szymon would dart like a fiery arrow from house to house, inspecting the *Shema* — the prayer nestled within the mezuzah — at the door of every home in our community.

Szymon's neighbour, Sonek the cartman, who lived in a shed with his wife and little girl, was a man of steel. People believed that Sonek could do with one hand what Samson had done to the Philistines with two. It was reputed that one rainy night, when his horse tripped and broke a leg, Sonek had picked up the beloved mare without blinking, brought her home to the stable, covered her with his own blanket and nursed the animal back to health. Since then he had never sat atop the cart.

Every day Sonek got up before the first spark of dawn, thanked God for his life of plenty and went off to the bakery where he worked as a delivery man. But on the night, the horrible night when the Almighty took his little girl away, Sonek ran out naked into the yard and, throwing his fists at the heavens, shouted: 'Murderer, murderer! What have You done? What have You done?' From that moment, he became a mocker of religion, a morbid man impossible to be with. Before long, his wife had to leave him and go back to her parents.

Well, to say that Sonek's blasphemous outpourings made him Szymon's mortal enemy would be an understatement.

And the feeling was mutual. Not surprisingly, when Szymon approached Sonek's doorstep, the cartman chased him away with his horsewhip. 'Sonek!' yelled the fanatical mystic. 'You'll burn in hell, I promise you!' 'Then at least,' the other shot back, 'after my bitter cold life, I'll be warm for a change!' At this, Szymon spat upon the ground, in the general direction of Sonek's feet, and ran off to find another doorstep.

Across from Szymon lived our caretaker, Stasiek, a small, bald, frisky man, with a pair of eyes as vacant as two muddy puddles, and a big yellow Franz Josef moustache under his red nose. Every Sunday after church Stasiek got drunk, cursed the Jews, beat his wife and dragged her back into his dwelling; after a half-hour of pleading for mercy, she would emerge with a satisfied smirk creasing her sharp features.

One Easter Sunday, when the sky was a blue, unblemished expanse and the snow was already thawing — though here and there the odd patch still fought for a few more minutes of white life — Stasiek entered the yard looking sombre and confused. He couldn't work out how it was possible for a pathetic consumptive like Szymon to have crucified the Son of his God. In any case, after downing half a bottle of vodka he decided that the criminal had to pay. Abruptly if unsteadily he burst into the evangelist's abode and, all the while shrieking 'Where is God's killer?', gave Szymon's terrified wife Doba and their two children a severe beating. She tried to plead with him: 'Stasiek, stop it, please, stop it. We haven't eaten for three days, Szymon is not here, he went out to try to borrow a few groshen to buy us a piece of bread.' But the caretaker had clearly taken leave of his senses; he was in a drunken, crazy trance, and quite unstoppable.

Suddenly, Stasiek spotted his intended victim about to enter the unlit corridor. He waited for Szymon in the shadows, then grabbed him from behind by his thin throat.

Szymon's face went blue and black, his bulging eyes seemed to mirror a final prayer, another second and he would be dead. But then a miracle. Out of nowhere Sonek appeared, picked up Stasiek like a chook, whirled him around his head three times, and tossed him like a rag doll out through the open window and into the mud outside. Still utterly composed, Sonek walked out without a word. However, while passing the bruised and bloodied local bouncer, he bent over until his face was almost pushing against Stasiek's. 'If I ever catch you touching Szymon with as much as a single finger, rest assured there won't be anything left of you for the gravedigger!'

A few minutes later Sonek returned carrying two warm loaves of bread under one arm and a bundle of dry wood under the other. As the fire in the dead stove began to sing, Sonek sat down to break bread with Szymon's battered family.

The following Friday, at the synagogue, Szymon imparted the whole incredible saga to a circle of open-mouthed fellow worshippers. When he had finished, one of them asked with a mischievous twinkle, 'And did you eventually find the proper *Shema* in Sonek's mezuzah?'

Szymon looked up and scratched his head. 'You know,' he said, 'last night I couldn't sleep, so I sneaked out of bed, quietly got dressed and went outside. It was pitch-black. Almost immediately I noticed a fine sliver of light moving about in the yard, and then I heard a voice that seemed to come from inside it — a voice like the wail of a fiddle. *Where are you off to, Szymon?* it asked. "In search of Sonek's *Shema*," I replied. And the beam of light answered: *Then seek within his heart.*'

❧ *A Social Function* ❧

I was fascinated by the inn and bordello that stood like a forbidden secret on the corner of Masarska and Limanowskiego. Although I had attempted to negotiate its threshold many a time, I was always unceremoniously rebuffed, evidently on account of my youth. My lucky break came when one of the damsels who worked there, 'Little Golden Hand' (so called because of her professional dexterity), accosted me in the street one day and entrusted me to deliver a verbal message to her fiancé, the underworld boss known as Blind Max, who happened to be on a business visit to the establishment.

Luckily, when I arrived Max was involved in a poker game, something at which no one would dare to disturb him, so they asked me to sit quietly in a corner and wait until the maestro was ready to appear out of the smoke. With thinly disguised enthusiasm, I agreed.

While waiting I observed several robust men around the counter; they had beady eyes, short necks and hands like steel shovels, and were downing vodka after vodka. From behind the thin walls I could hear the moans of industrious females and the curses and grunts of husky males. I thought I was caught in a scene from Sergiusz Piasecki's classic novel, *Lover of the Great Bear*, where men read the stars like skilled navigators, saw right through a deck of cards with grey eagle eyes, and knew exactly when and when not to draw. Then I imagined women with hefty hips and muscular arms, throwing men ceiling-high and letting them land on their sizzling bellies and roast to death...

The staff of this specialty house were all Jewish, but its guests — wayfarers, removalists — were a rather multicultural brotherhood. Perhaps it was thanks to the common purpose shared by these two groups that the Jewish customers were tipped off. They learnt that a gang of hooligans armed with knives, sticks and iron gloves was determined, on the coming Green (Maundy) Thursday, to restore 'holy order' in our exclusively Jewish quarter. On the appointed day, singing lustily, the hellbent disciples boarded the evening tram that travelled from Bałucki Rynek through the Jewish district. Just before reaching Masarska Street, these hoodlums, holding to an almost military formation, abruptly disembarked — and to their unpleasant surprise were confronted by a forest of Jewish toughs, their steel fists eager for a fight!

There was another remarkable thing about this incident. In the land of my birth, whenever defenceless Jews were being beaten up, you couldn't spot a policeman for miles; yet on this occasion, within seconds the official guardians of the law had descended on our area like a swarm of black mosquitoes, and thus prevented the order-makers from receiving a thorough thrashing.

In a matter of days a rumour circulated that the audacity of those steel fists might force the authorities to close down our homely institution. However, at the last moment it was miraculously saved through the intervention of the altruistic police commissioner, who sagaciously pointed out the brothel's undeniable value and the social function it performed.

Now more than ever I revisit, in my imaginings, my city of the waterless river. I walk for hours through the empty, eerie streets in search of a familiar face that isn't there. The once secretive door of the bordello inn stands wide open and Little Golden Hand sits by a table draped with a red tablecloth. 'They murdered my Max, and everybody else,' she cries. 'They're gone… all gone.'

'Then what is keeping *you* here?' I ask her. 'Why not leave this desolate place and join them?'

'Not yet,' she answers. 'I'm waiting for you to forget me.'

❧ *The Assistant* ❧

Adjoining the timber yard just along from our block stood a
small wooden dwelling. It harboured two shops: a fruiterer and
a plumber. The plumber's was perhaps not bigger than three
metres by five, yet it contained a workbench, a small table, three
chairs and two beds — one for the plumber Zygmunt Szulc and
his wife Fernanda, the other for their nineteen-year-old assistant, Meir. This young man was an orphan who had arrived
from a nearby township carrying a brown suitcase. Despite his
perpetually mournful demeanour, Meir was forever cajoling me
(unsuccessfully, I might add) to accompany him on one of his
regular visits to a prostitute.

Zygmunt was not actually a plumber, but since he worked
with tin and there was no exact Yiddish term to describe his
profession, that was how he was known. The Szulces were
Jewish, but because of their dark skin, outlandish ways and
peculiar solitary existence, we called them 'the Moors'.

A tall, slender, laid-back fellow in his early fifties, with a
pair of hands that reached well below his knees, Zygmunt was
a master tradesman in the production of coach-lanterns. Fernanda was in her mid-forties, vivacious, plump, with sweaty skin
and fiery eyes; she wore a red scarf on her thick neck, and a huge
gold ring dangled from each of her earlobes.

I don't know how, but before long I had befriended Meir,
four years my senior, and virtually overnight he became my
trusted mentor. In secret, Meir told me that the lanterns he
and Zygmunt produced were attached to black coaches belonging to the upper nobility; that sometimes, when a baron, a
knight or even a prince pulled in to replace a lantern, he,
Meir, would glimpse through the partly-drawn curtains of
the coach a beautiful naked young girl lying across the plush
seat. This and other graphic accounts, especially those about

Fernanda's nightly doings, set my imagination aflame and enriched my sleep with joyous, uplifting dreams.

One Sunday evening, after a hefty dinner, Zygmunt went to bed and never got up again. Fernanda screamed, slapped his face, pleaded, cried her heart out — 'Zygmunt, Zygmunt, how can you do this to me!' — but it was all in vain. After the seven customary days of mourning, the assistant took over his master's role, and, like a river diverted by an earthquake, his life assumed a new and much-altered course. Fernanda seemed pleased with his work, as was Meir with her motherly care. While she was serving breakfast one morning, she mentioned matter-of-factly that she intended to increase turnover and bring in more stock, and since the place was quite small she might as well dispose of the unnecessary extra bed. Meir nodded; he had always been an obedient assistant.

However, out of the blue, fate took a snipe at this cosiness, for the industry of wagging tongues forced Fernanda to bid an abrupt farewell to our neighbourhood. As for Meir, I don't know what became of him — perhaps he went the way of many people at that time: to the East. Clutching the same brown suitcase he'd arrived with, the sad orphan with nowhere to go departed from our lives, never to be seen again. But his image still lingers on in the chambers of my fading memory like a bashful smile on a mourner's face.

≈ *Miscarried Revolution* ≈

Ideologically speaking, our school was Bundist, and distinctly non-Zionist. A return to the land of the prophets was not our dream, but rather to make prophetic the land of our present. And although we were not a religious school, we were all (as father would have said) very much circumcised at heart.

My noble friend Haim, incurable dreamer, his mane of sun-burnt hair hanging over his thickly rimmed glasses, who would have given anyone the shirt off his back, was a misfit in either camp. Perhaps it had to do with his idiosyncratic personality, or maybe with his life at home — a sick mother whom I remember as a white moon sinking above a twilit horizon, and a despairing father who couldn't make ends meet.

Haim knew Marx, Engels and Bakunin before I knew the alphabet, though it was not on account of his erudition that he was known at school as 'The Professor', but because of the spectacles. And yes, our Professor worshipped Marx and his apostles. Once, in the middle of a geometry lesson, he rose up like a stormy red flag. 'It's not Archimedes' law,' he declared, 'that should be taught at school, but Marx's sociopolitical *science* — a science that will bring the revolution and inaugurate the benevolent socialist state, which will restore health to all sick mothers and release all working-class fathers from their daily miseries.'

How was Haim — the lover of Jewish history who was pounding on the gates of the impossible — to know, in those heady days of socialist fever, that Marx had been a self-hating Jew whose *Zur Judenfrage* ('On the Jewish Question'), written in 1843, was to become a handbook for European anti-semitism? How, for that matter, was he to know that revolutions change nothing, but merely replace one tyrant with another?

And yet, it was perhaps thanks to his very innocence that he survived. Because at the first sign of trouble in his home-land, Haim — fired with the strains of the *Internationale*, his heart still throbbing with Stalin's exploits — took the road, the one paved with broken glass, to the motherland of his dreams. Alas, how quickly he learnt that a lie can be fashioned into an evil god!

Luckily he came back alive, and time would take care of his feet, frostbitten and bloodied from their misadventure. But the soul of this outrageously, incorrigibly romantic man never stopped bleeding.

☞ *Summer Camp* ☜

In my early teens I joined the Jewish youth movement known as Skif. The word was an acronym for *Sotsyalistisher Kinder Farband* (Socialist Children's Union); the movement dreamt of a perfect reality, of a world where children would be regarded not merely as children but as young people with equal rights.

Naturally, when we spoke about camp in those days, we had in mind tents and summer holidays — what else? In July–August 1936, while the intrepid freedom-fighters in Spain battled valiantly for their liberty, we, the children of Skif, were enjoying our summer camp in a valley not far from Vilna under the banner *Red Spain*. It was known as Skif's 'Tenth Socialist Children's Republic'.

This had originally been intended as an international event; we expected Polish and German contingents of Red Scouts to join us, at least in proclaiming our children's state. But as it turned out, the Poles and the Germans were unable to make the journey. Yet we, the two hundred or so Jewish boys and girls, were not deterred, and with tremendous gusto we upheld the international spirit of our Republic. At morning roll-call, we working-class children who spent our days in poverty and squalor stood radiantly in a huge circle, in our blue shirts and red ties, singing:

Take our hands, sisters, brothers,
Raise the flags heaven-high;
Let our freedom song resound,
Let our voices reach the sky.

Let our freedom song re-echo,
Let us walk hand in hand;
Wherever brothers sing together
The whole wide world is fatherland.

I remember the day the floodgates of the sky broke open, and our white tents could not protect us from the sudden turn in the weather. Drenched to the bone, we crammed into a nearby barn, where, clinging to each other for warmth, we burst forth in song. At nightfall, the storm having subsided, each of us took a dry piece of timber from the barn and we sat around the fire to listen to a speaker.

He spoke late into the night, shaping his every word with great care, and each of his sentences had a vividness, a coherence, that showed beyond doubt how it was all up to *us* if we wanted to bring to fruition our dream of a perfect reality. As I took hold of my hoped-for girlfriend's hand, I noticed the full moon's esoteric smile. In the diary of my mind I quietly noted the special feeling of that moment — a mental note I have never to this day forgotten.

➾ *Traumas* ➾

At the threshold of what would be the last year of my formal education, I had to change schools. I was nearly fifteen. Father couldn't take any more of my rascally, unruly behaviour and my academic negligence, which practically every week saw him summoned to my principal's office. Enough was enough, he said, and enrolled me in the local state school for Jewish boys. The change was quite traumatic. On several mornings, walking in a daze, I actually found myself, to my own bewilderment, in front of the gates of my former school!

My new principal, Szelupski, was a medium-built man with soft brown eyes and a flat, greying moustache under his slightly crooked nose. 'You have to repeat grade six,' he told me, politely enough. I asked him why. 'Because I have no great faith in your Yiddish schooling.' After adding a few words about my former headmaster, whom he seemed to admire, Szelupski led me into my prospective classroom, where in front of some forty students Miss Maler, teacher of literature and language, set about interrogating me.

'Do you speak Polish at home?' was her first question.

'No, Miss.'

'Oh, how awful. Do you read Polish books?'

'Yes,' I whispered.

'Well,' said the gentle Miss Maler, who, like most of the teachers at the school, was Jewish. 'I was led to believe that your school reads only Yiddish books… So tell us, young man, what do you like most in our Polish literature?'

'Mickiewicz,' I answered, still whispering.

'Excellent,' she exclaimed, 'he's my favourite writer too. And as it happens, he is next on our reading list. Perhaps you would like to inform your new friends which book by Mickiewicz you like best. You might even treat us,' she continued with an ironic smile, 'to a line or two from this great work.'

I don't know why, but I didn't respond to the first part of Miss Maler's request. Instead, I began to recite from memory 'The Year 1812', the eleventh book of *Pan Tadeusz*… and didn't stop until the bell for recess shook my new teacher of Polish literature out of her state of mesmerized amazement. 'Is that what they teach in your Yiddish school?' she asked at last, shaking her well-groomed head.

'Yes,' I said.

As she showed me to my desk, I heard her mutter: 'If only they would stop speaking that dreadful language at home.'

After dinner that evening I related the whole episode to my father. He was visibly upset. Obviously, the teacher's assimilationist sentiments had made him realize that taking his son out of the Yiddish-speaking school had been a mistake. It was now too late to remedy it.

'Why do they dislike Yiddish so much?' I asked him.

'Well, it's in the nature of the assimilators. Actually, it's not the language — it's the people who speak it they abhor.'

'Would that change if we all spoke Polish?'

'No. Unfortunately, this is an ongoing historical trauma. Such characters are basically ashamed of their own people.'

Later, as night lost its fear of the dark and the stove died in a whisper, I dreamt that I was back at my old school. The history teacher was praising my work, praising how deftly I had paraphrased a parable of Rabbi Akiva's:

On the banks of a sparkling river walks the mighty emperor Hadrian, enemy of the teaching of Torah. He is imploring the Hebrew-speaking fishes to join him, in a celebration of life, on the grassy banks of the sparkling river…

❧ *Karinka* ❧

We belonged to the same movement, Skif. She, at fifteen, was already twenty-five. A blonde with an elongated face, olive skin and deep serious eyes, she was proud and incomprehensibly fickle. A whole universe of boys, including me, was madly in love with her. And Karinka? Possessed of a nonchalant sensuality, she loved us all but cared for none of us.

One midnight, in the Tatra mountains, at a summer camp in the village of Bundówki near Zakopane, I was privileged to stand guard with her. The night was cold, so we kept each other warm talking about socialism and free love. Karinka was sweet and evasive, but as the moonlight fell on her face she appeared to me like a teasing Madonna. Languishing in the dark, I asked her: 'Why do you break so many hearts?' 'To make them complete,' she said. Then she placed her warm lips to my eager ear and murmured:

> 'The grass was wet with dew,
> The well stood deep in thought;
> He made love to me,
> I loved, and loved him not.'

At that moment we heard footsteps — a change of guard. We parted and walked off to our respective lodgings. At morning roll-call, *my* Karinka gave me a strange look, as if to ask: *Who are you, boy? Have we ever met?*

On the train journey home we travelled, not by accident, in the same compartment. I sat by the window and she stretched herself out on the seat, placing her beautiful head on my lap. It was night and most of the others were fast asleep. She allowed me to kiss her lips, slide my hand behind her bra, fondle her paradise apples, fresh from the very tree of life.

In that autumn of 1937, Karinka became a student in a girls' high school, and I became a furrier's apprentice. This situation placed us on two different planets. But three years later, at the beginning of the end, I ran into her again. She was carrying two buckets of water and seemed distraught. I wanted to help but she pushed me away. 'Don't you dare come near me,' she cried.

I discovered later that poverty, hunger and loneliness had forced her to marry a smallish man twenty years her senior.

Apparently he was high up in the service of our inverted ghetto-state. It was rumoured that he had previously been employed in a girls' high school as an instructor in moral behaviour.

My heart pined for Karinka but there was nothing I could do — except dream that she had agreed to run away with me, though there would have been nowhere to run. So my might-have-been beloved vanished from my horizon like the wistful smoke from a passing steamer. But to this day, it hasn't stopped hovering before my dimming eyes.

❧ *The Climb* ❧

The summer camp we set up in 1937 at Bundówki was within view of Giewont, the highest mountain in the land of our birth. Our leaders were Miss Muster, Niemele Libeskind and Juda Kersh, assisted by the tall willowy silverbirch-pale Nono Goldman, the brave Geniek Boczkowski — much respected because at sixteen he was already shaving his chin — and the incorruptible Bono Winer, my underground cell leader in those days without years.

At morning roll-call we hoisted our Red Falcons flag, and with songs dedicated to universal brotherhood we began our daily activities. Not far from us, the ND — the xenophobic National Democrats — had established their own camp head-quarters. Apparently, songs of eternal brotherhood were not much to their taste, and in response to our efforts they strung up on their flagpole the effigy of a Jew, with a big red sign that read: THIS IS OUR ANSWER TO THE PROVOCATIONS OF THE JEWISH COLONY.

For days we enthusiastically prepared ourselves for our excursion up the famous Kasprowy Wierch. We knew this was a rather dangerous undertaking, since the ascent of the mountain up to the plateau at the summit was precipitous, the traffic was strictly one-way, and the climb was possible only with the aid of iron hooks and chains.

When we reached the foot of the mountain, Bono and his inseparable friend Nono assumed leadership of the climb. The rear was covered by the aforementioned Geniek. The hot, humid day made our task arduous, yet we continued undeterred; even the ten-year-olds among us kept up the pace.

As our forward detachment came into sight of the plateau, we were signalled to stop. A reception committee of three ND thugs was up ahead, blocking our progress! The heat by this time was unbearable; the sun's rays, like burning lances, pierced our bodies — which hung perilously in the air. Our boys at the top pleaded, 'Please, there are young kids amongst us, you may cause casualties.' 'We don't care,' they retorted. 'Who wants you here, anyway!' Just as the standoff was becoming critical, a woman who happened to be walking up on the plateau noticed our predicament. 'You let those people through,' she shouted, 'or I'll call the police.'

Two hours later, as we entered the Valley of Five Lakes, we spotted our three friends once again, and approached them. 'We want a word with you,' Bono Winer said. 'What about?' asked the oldest among them, an expression of lazy boredom on his face. 'About your nastiness, pal,' came the reply — and Bono hurled his fist into the hoodlum's face. It sent them all packing.

Intent on vengeance, they visited us later, in the middle of the night. Much to their unpleasant surprise, however, we expected them and were ready, waiting.

The following morning, right after breakfast, Juda Kersh deftly took the stand at our timber-constructed 'radio station' and began his broadcast. 'Hallo hallo,' he announced. 'This is the free voice of the Eleventh Socialist Children's Republic in the district of Zakopane. Greetings to all people of goodwill on our planet Earth!'

Antisemitism, he announced, was a dying weed with many ugly roots, but we, the Jewish people, together with all mankind, would uproot this monstrous chimera. Arm in arm, we were marching, marching towards a new dawn...

Unfortunately, dear Juda, those days without years proved your prophecy a little premature.

⇜ *Chessgame* ⇝

The life of Dr Igor Alekseyevich, who befriended my father, reads like an outlandish piece of fiction. His own father had been conscripted into the Tsar's army at the age of ten, and celebrated his twentieth birthday in 1877, while marching under the leadership of Duke Nikolai against the Turks. After a fierce battle, for which he was later decorated, Igor's father was taken prisoner; he escaped, but was quickly caught and condemned to be shot. Standing blindfolded before the firing-squad, begging God for a miracle, he suddenly heard the gallop of hoofs. It was said that a beautiful maiden named Emilia, of the noble Sephardic lineage of Gracia Nasi, arrived on a white horse, freed the condemned man for a pot of gold, and became his wife and Igor's mother.

At the time of his barmitzvah Igor's family emigrated to Germany, where the boy completed his medical studies with great distinction and (having become a Bismarckian true believer) was quickly catapulted to the pinnacle of his profession, with the highest circles seeking his services. However, as the 1930s advanced — a time when God's bank went into voluntary receivership and all promissory notes lost their validity — Igor found himself prohibited from practising, and eventually was dispatched with thousands of other Jews to the muddy Polish border town of Zbąszyn. Soon afterwards he turned up in the city of the waterless river.

Every Sunday afternoon at exactly four o'clock, Dr Igor would appear with Germanic punctuality at our doorstep, to play a game of chess with my father and talk about Judaism, which to him meant '*Die Bibel*'. Igor could not accept father's premise that we Jews were a nation: 'This, Herr Gershon,' he would say, '*ist ein grosser Irrtum*, a great mistake. We are no more than a religious community, that's all.'

'Well,' father would counter, making his next move on the chessboard between them, 'the Bible will resolutely disagree with you.'

If the doctor was taken aback he was not inclined to contradict father, who had studied for years in a yeshiva. But after a tactical sip of the fresh tea that mother served, he responded at last. 'Yes,' he said, 'that may be so. But how then do you explain Lev Tolstoy's dictum that the Jew — not the Jewish nation! — is "that sacred being who has brought down from heaven the everlasting fire, and has illumined with it the entire world"?'

'I don't know, Igor, I haven't come across Tolstoy's dictum,' father replied. 'But maybe what this great thinker meant was that our father Abraham was the first to proclaim the idea of *Achad*, the One, the harmony of our universe. This became the fundamental principle of all the sciences, both known and as yet unknown — and of all art, literature, and sane theology.'

'And what may be the essence of your *sane theology*, Herr Gershon?'

'Perhaps,' said father with a spark in his eye, 'that this world of ours will have a meaning, and a secure future, only when all people learn to be in love with *Achad*. When that day comes, the practice of religion will be regarded as an offence...'

And concluding his next move with a flourish of his wrist, father announced: 'By the way, Herr Doctor, it's checkmate.'

❦ *A Scandal* ❦

After leaving school and spending a few unsatisfactory months with a furrier, I was apprenticed to a tailor, a certain Mr Henry Brawerbaum. He was a stocky, droop-shouldered man in his early fifties, with long arms that appeared to hang limp at his sides, and in his sallow face rested a pair of eyes like two razor slits. Yet Henry — who could easily have played the role of Hugo's famous hunchback, Quasimodo — was a noble human being who enjoyed a reputation as one of the best tailors in town.

His wife, Marieta, was a small blonde, possibly in her late thirties. She had broad hips and a high bosom, incessantly pursed her painted lips, and sauntered about the house like a French perfumery. Needless to say, she was Henry's icon, though why she had married him was an enigma.

They lived in the better part of our city of the waterless river, in a two-bedroom apartment. There was also a kitchen, its walls tiled in green and white and its ceiling painted beige, and it was here that Henry had set up his workroom. His senior employee, Sasha, who knew the outcome of all things in advance and finished every sentence with 'I told you so', had come from a little township with his young wife. He was an excellent tailor and a good-looking man, with a mulatto's complexion, wavy hair and black eyes that brimmed with wonder — a wonder which Marieta was determined to investigate. The third workman in the atelier was the ever-silent and inconspicuous presser, Felek.

On the first day of my employment, Mr Brawerbaum took me aside. 'Young man,' he stated rather solemnly, 'one of your duties as an apprentice will be to assist the lady of the house with domestic chores, if she should need you.' I was of course delighted with such a prospect and immediately began to fantasize.

On Mondays our boss would leave the house right after breakfast. It was the day he had reserved for buying materials and trimmings, and for enjoying a lunch with his colleagues in the trade. On one such Monday soon after I began there, I noticed Marieta winking Sasha over (I wished it could have been me) into the adjoining bedroom. Overcome with curiosity, I edged closer to the wooden stud wall.

'Please, darling,' I heard her address him in Polish, 'don't torment me.'

'Stop it, Marieta!' Sasha adored the good-hearted Quasimodo, and he sounded frightened. 'You have a husband, a gentleman, who loves you dearly, and you want to betray him?'

'Oh, you silly boy,' Marieta retorted. 'To love is much, much mightier than to be loved!'

'No, Marieta!' Sasha declared firmly. 'And don't speak to me in Polish.'

'Oh, Sasha, sweetie. Yiddish is so unromantic!'

But Sasha turned on his heel, banged the bedroom door behind him and came through into the workroom. He was pale and sweating, and clearly agitated. The presser Felek gave him a dirty look. At that instant I heard Marieta call *my* name.

'Don't go in there!' Sasha hissed.

I stopped, then remembered Henry's injunction that I should respond if his wife called on me. I opened the bedroom door and paused just beyond the threshold, paralysed.

Marieta stood there like Eve before her enlightenment by the snake. As if by magic, the door slid shut behind me.

'What are you waiting for, you fool!' she screamed. 'Can't you see I have a sore hand? Help me — I can't reach around behind my back!' And she hurled her bra furiously in my face. Just then the bedroom door flew open, and there was Mr Brawerbaum.

'What's this!' my boss shouted. 'What's going on here?'

Marieta didn't skip a beat as she explained, with a giggle, the reason for my presence.

'Wait outside,' her husband commanded curtly.

I obeyed, and while waiting I heard more giggles from Marieta, along with Quasimodo's heart-wrenching pleas and entreaties. After a few minutes he quietly re-emerged, gave me my unearned pay for the rest of the month, and, almost in a whisper, said: 'Please go. Go into the workroom, take your things, and never come back again.'

As I collected my few belongings I heard Sasha murmur, 'I told you so.'

Three weeks later I unexpectedly met up with Sasha — on a new job. I was astounded. 'Sasha!' I cried. 'What happened?'

'That woman was Potiphar's wife incarnate,' he replied. 'And I, unfortunately, lacked the strength of Joseph.'

≈ *On the Slope* ≈

Time had embarked on a precipitous, irreversible journey, roller-coasting along the brink of a fathomless abyss. A smouldering breeze from the west brought evil tidings. Newspapers, radio and the politicians screamed: *War is imminent!* Yet the government in the land of my birth was more concerned with devoting all its energies to the Jewish question.

One million Jews must go! — to Madagascar, Palestine, Uganda. Janina Prystorowa, a reactionary member of the Sejm (the Polish parliament), in conjunction with her colleague, Father Stanisław Trzeciak, proposed in 1936 that *shechitah*, the ritual kosher slaughter of cattle, contradicted Christian ethics and should be prohibited on the grounds of cruelty.

If this bill became law, argued our city's *Kehila*, the Jewish council on which the anti-religious Bund held a majority at the time, it would not only infringe on the religious beliefs of the Jewish communities, but threaten their very livelihood. Clearly, as in all such cases, the whole thing was just another ploy of the antisemites, a smokescreen for their devilish intentions. After some deliberations a national strike was proclaimed, a strike that would bring all industry, commerce and education in our country to a total standstill.

I vividly recall the day of the general strike, 17 September 1937. The Jewish quarters were galvanized, and the foreboding whisper of an unbelievable daring, fraught with great danger, hovered in the air. Groups of Bundist militia waited concealed in nooks and shadows, prepared to respond to any provocation, while the mounted police, their presence visible and their bayonets fixed, patrolled the streets, ready to protect the local hooligans.

But as the day negotiated its last traces of light, and evening dropped like an impatient drape, and the slanting dimness of the forest of puffed-out factory chimneys resumed its cheerless eternal vigil, my heart sank. I watched the Bundist militia leave their stations for home, watched the mounted police disperse, and my disappointment was complete. I, the fifteen-year-old revolutionary, felt cheated. The general strike that I had hoped would lead our people to the barricades had fizzled out like a punctured balloon.

Dejected, I made my way home; but on turning a corner I came face to face with a small procession of people carrying a tall wooden cross and shouting slogans into the air. I stopped to watch, and as the cross passed by, one of the zealous marchers ripped off my woollen school cap and screamed: 'We'll do to the Jews what they do to our cattle!' He was joined by the others, and they all chanted in unison. 'We'll do to the Jews what they do to our cattle! We'll do to the Jews what they do to our cattle! So help us God!'

And they did.

☙ *Hotza-tza* ☙

Little Itzik, whom we called the Barber of Bałuty, was an aggressive leader and the acknowledged poet of the young Communists. He was constantly at loggerheads with his neighbour Bainisz, a Bundist and mechanic whom he both respected and hated. 'I respect you, Bainisz,' he said, 'for your brave stand against the antisemites… And hate you,' he screamed, poking a finger into his neighbour's face, 'for your counter-revolutionary activities. Just wait, you Social Fascist,' Itzik boiled. 'After our revolution, we will deal with your kind.'

The last municipal election here was like a war, albeit one in which nobody was actually killed. There were fights, to be sure, crude fights; but most of the confrontations were verbal. I recall little Itzik standing like a featherless rooster in front of Zombkowski's pharmacy on Limanowskiego Street, his Adam's apple jumping nervily up and down in his scraggy throat. The night before, he had engaged in another vitriolic exchange with his neighbour, who had dared to brand his beloved Stalin as Ivan the Terrible Incarnate; now Itzik was paying him back:

My Bundist neighbour has a scheme
Hotza-tza, hotza-tza
To go into partnership with Berlin
Hotza-tza, hotza-tza.

Now he spreads his toxic lore
Hotza-tza, tza hotza-tza
My neighbour is a hopeless bore
Hotza-tza, tza hotza-tza.

Sadly, it was not Bainisz's but rather Itzik's comrades who went into partnership with Berlin. A week after the real war broke out, the city of the waterless river was invaded. Next day Itzik, a small suitcase dangling from his hand, appeared on his neghbour's threshold. 'I am prepared to forgive you, Bainisz,' he announced. 'Let's go, we have no time to lose.'

'Where to, Itzik, where to?'

'To the land of the Volga, of course — to the land of freedom and brotherhood. Remember what even your own Social Fascist newspaper, the *Naye Folkstsaytung*, once wrote? Bertrand Russell was visiting Moscow and asked an ordinary worker "Why don't you take your holidays abroad?" "Because," the man replied, "I don't want to lose even a week of living in our glorious country!"'

In the end Itzik managed to persuade his old adversary and they went off to the East together, though circumstances eventually drew them apart and they lost contact with each other. In October 1943, in the company of a military officer, Bainisz was sent beyond the Urals to repair some equipment. Their train broke down just outside a gulag ('a camp for dangerous enemies of our state,' the officer explained, though Bainisz didn't need any explanations). They would have to spend several days at the camp, since the next train was almost a week away.

One can picture Bainisz's astonishment when, as he walked through this camp of dangerous enemies of the state, he spotted little Itzik, lying uncovered and miserable on a wooden bunk in the freezing night. 'Itzik!' he called. 'Itzik, is that you?' His former neighbour stared at Bainisz in disbelief. Bainisz wore a woollen uniform coat, fur hat, high boots, and seemed to be well fed. 'Why are you here, Itzik?' he persisted. 'What have you done to deserve this?'

'Bainisz,' the other replied at last. 'I can see that you are in the company of a high officer. Maybe you can help me.'

A while later Bainisz returned to Itzik's bunk with a pot of hot thick soup and a black sweater. 'That's all I can do for you. But tell me, Itzik, what crime did you commit?'

'I mentioned to my foreman,' the poet stuttered through his soup, 'that the lice were eating me up. The foreman reported this to the authorities, who were convinced it was a metaphor for something else.'

In August 1946, right after the Kielce pogrom, Bainisz returned to the city of his birth. There, to his joy, he discovered little Itzik again, reborn in a white jacket and standing in front of his barber shop. 'Itzik, thank God you made it!' he cried.

'Yes, and so did you,' his old enemy replied. 'Thanks to the East.'

Over coffee, Bainisz made it known that he would shortly be leaving for America. Itzik was unimpressed. 'You shouldn't go, Bainisz, you shouldn't. We're building a new life here, a new order.'

'Yes, complete with pogroms,' Bainisz retorted. 'Tell me, is there any other land in Europe where Jews are still being murdered after the war?'

Itzik didn't answer. But next morning, when Bainisz dropped by his shop to say goodbye, the old poet was ready for him:

The American Imperialists are a pest
Hotza-tza, hotza-tza
For spies and snakes a rotten nest
Hotza-tza, hotza-tza.

Over there things are harder
Hotza-tza, tza hotza-tza
Stalin is still our beloved Father
Hotza-tza, tza hotza-tza.

❧ *A Chat* ❧

Sergey Nutkiewicz, our tutor in political economy during our
school days, was a corpulent five-footer on short legs. In defi-
ance of nature's unkindness, he carried his frame with great
dignity and resoluteness. He had a face like the open book of
an illustrious spirit, a pair of big sad blue eyes, and a velvet
voice that drove the fairer sex to distraction. He was a leading
Bundist in our city of the waterless river, but much more a
Fabian than a fanatic.

We would meet many years after the war, at the tail-end of
a beautiful summer. Sergey was already rich in seasons but still
very much awake. We sat in a little garden, sipping black coffee
across a marble table. The warm afternoon breeze played havoc
with the last three grey hairs on his head. We sat for a good
while before I finally broke the silence.

'I recall one of your talks — to a group of us, when we'd
already left school. It was in the late thirties, after the Moscow
purges…'

Sergey was stunned. 'Really? How can you remember a thing like that?'

'Well, Sergey, the gods have endowed me with a long memory — which by the way is not always a blessing.'

He smiled, still shaking his head.

'Yes, this may sound incredible to you,' I went on, 'but I can still hear, in vivid detail, your emphatic avowal of the importance of a strong socialist brotherhood, of the unity of mankind. And how, in the wake of the Moscow trials, you said: "History may for once contradict nature. I think the time has arrived for the sun to rise in the west."

'Well, it seems to me,' I continued, 'that this will never come to pass. Not only are western skies too narrow for your rising sun, but the ideal of a united humanity has surely been killed off at the roots.'

Sergey wrinkled his brow, and as his sad blue eyes scanned my face, I could sense how carefully he was composing his thoughts. I waited, and this time it was he who broke the silence.

'Dulcinea del Toboso never existed, my friend,' said Sergey. 'Don Quixote de la Mancha dreamt her up. Yet for his Dulcinea he was ready to lay down his life.'

➳ *The Spaniard* ➳

One of the most colourful personalities in our microcosm was the mystic seer, Ezro the Spaniard. I had a great regard for the man's exuberant fancy. I loved to listen to his buoyant, often arcane stories, and to his claim of being a direct descendant of Abraham Ibn Ezra, that marvellous twelfth-century scholar, traveller and hero of many a legendary tale.

Our own Ezro's outlandish approach to life obliged him to live outside the cultural perimeter of our community. People could not accept the fact that he called his old shack 'Andalusia', that he wore his long black hair in a ponytail, and that he sported a gold ring in his right earlobe. Then there was his needle-thin moustache, his sideboards like two meticulously shaped sickles that ran almost into the corners of his mouth, and, on top of that, his habit of going about, even on the hottest days, in a black woollen ankle-length coat adorned with a brown fur collar.

At the beginning of 1939, on a day that had already shed its afternoon, Ezro my fanciful friend waved me over. 'Psst, hey, young fellow, would you care to step into Andalusia for a moment or two?' Ezro looked unusually secretive. After a tense pause he announced resolutely: 'I'm going away at daybreak.'

I was stunned. 'Why?' I almost shouted.

'Ezro is a restless man,' he replied, 'and must leave his tent and rejoin the road from time to time, perhaps for his own wellbeing.'

'Sir, I don't understand.'

'You soon will...'

'But where will you go?' I persisted.

'I don't know.'

'You mean you're going to... nowhere?'

'No,' Ezro shook his head. 'A man who *has* nowhere in his heart cannot *go* there. How can he be in something, when that very something is in him?'

By now I was utterly confused.

'Existence,' he went on, 'is but a passing phenomenon. Ours is only the present, of which we comprehend nothing. Our future may well be an illusion, and our past is in love with oblivion, which enables us to repeat our follies with a smile.'

I nodded absently, but he had well and truly lost me.

'I once heard of a prophet,' Ezro continued, 'the homeliest of all prophets. Yet his life was an eternal rendezvous with legend, and likewise with dreams — one without the other would make no sense, this prophet said. As for me, I love exile, because in exile I can hear God's cry. He cries over his worshippers' stupidity: they don't realize that their foolishness is their own worst enemy.'

He stopped to take a breath, then began to pack his belongings. 'The road is longing for my footfall,' he declared.

Bewildered, I looked up into his face.

'Well,' said the mystic, pointing at the skyline. 'You will see how our vistas are consumed in flames. Soon there will be only ashes left...' A profound sadness had entered his eyes, and seemed to colour his deep voice. 'It's time for me to go, my friend,' he announced, and his meaning was clear again. I shook my head, but Ezro merely smiled.

'Time to go,' he repeated, 'in search of the thing which does not exist.'

≈ The Last Summer ≈

Early on the morning of 12 August 1939, as the mist cleared — though a few patches still lingered, making our street more distant and unreal — mother called out: 'Quickly, go to the village where Pola and Frumetl are staying.' My sister and little niece were on a summer break in the nearby countryside. 'Help them pack up their belongings. Hurry! There's no time to lose, we're on the brink of war!'

As if to himself, father murmured: 'You spend a lifetime spinning dreams, and in the end you have to face a crude reality. Mankind,' he added quite audibly, 'can't control its own destiny. We are forever the cause, the tool, and the tragic casualty.'

The village was only an hour's tram-ride out of town, and from there the walk to the hamlet took a good thirty minutes.

I made my way through a dense forest of rustling pines, over green clearings sprinkled with yellow wildflowers, across fields of rippling corn. I advanced amid a stillness, except for the cornstalks' dreaded whisper of a premature harvest, of a life prickly as thistles.

I arrived just before noon. My sister was already packing, assisted by her host, the old German, Kling. A clever, kind-hearted man with an unsteady gait, Herr Kling was a wealthy farmer, owner of miles and miles of fertile land, hundreds of cattle and countless fowl. In the centre of his yard, besieged by random archipelagos of moss, stood a circular whitewashed well. I remember its freezing water, even on the hottest days, and the wooden bucket humming on its rusty iron chain.

As we finished packing I heard Kling remark: 'War is stupid, Herr Hitler is a madman.' But the farmer's son Ludwig, who each evening after a hefty meal would sit under the linden tree and play *Für Elise* on his trumpet, disagreed. 'Father,' he argued, 'you don't understand our brothers in the west, their lack of *Lebensraum*. The Führer's intention to annex the east, and there-by bring to fruition Germany's historical dreams, is a very wise one.'

The next day, sitting for dinner around our table with Pola and Frumetl, I repeated to my father the conversation I had overheard at farmer Kling's. 'What a grotesque absurdity!' he exclaimed. 'What pathetic, juvenile arrogance! A leader might have an idea of how and where a war begins, but never how and where it will end.'

Late at night we all went next door and congregated around our neighbour's Telefunken. 'This is Radio Berlin,' the loud-speaker crackled. '*Guten Tag, meine Damen und Herren*. We are repeating excerpts from our Führer's daily address.' Then the hated, distinctive voice. '*Die Juden*,' it thundered, and it was the hollow barking of a mad dog. '*Die Juden werden nicht mehr lachen!...*' When the speaker made some arrogant reference to Polish territory, I observed father's reaction: his face had turned grey. 'We are facing difficult times,' he said.

'Reb Gershon,' replied our deeply religious neighbour, Zilberszac, 'keep in mind that, since the beginning of time, Jews and hope have been interchangeable. Keep in mind our mighty God, and His Messiah. In days like these, even a Jew who does not believe in an Anointed One is not absolved from nevertheless believing that he is on his way.'

Father smiled, not just because he could not share our neighbour's faith, but because he loved this Talmudic twist. And out of respect to Zilberszac's opinion, naive though he regarded it, he preferred to end the exchange by shrugging his shoulders and remaining silent, rather than arguing and trying to disprove the other's abstractions.

A few days later, on a morning brimming with light and hope, I watched with pride as the intrepid Polish cavalry rode through our street. And I, a boy of seventeen, thought: Is there any power in the world that can measure up to this? Never!... Little could I know that the brilliant morning light was already infested with darkness, hope was already riddled with despair, and fate had propelled us on a journey of no return.

☙ *Patch of Light* ☙

Isaiah, son of Amoz, come down from your azure throne and see how the city of the waterless river celebrates, on this scorching August day, your beautiful vision. See how Poles and Jews, with spades and pickaxes in their hands, march shoulder to shoulder, singing songs, digging defensive trenches together against the oncoming common enemy. See how the little babushkas run from post to post with buckets of fresh water,

quenching the thirst of Jews; see how pious chassids in traditional black garb, with resolute curly sidelocks, and their
women in solemn wigs and with Sabbath blessings on their
lips, wipe the sweat off the brows of Polish men with crucifixes
dangling over hairy chests. Oh, how can one forget that patch
of light, that moment of brotherhood, of those unforgettable
summer days in August 1939?

I was digging near my school friend, Josef Wiesenfeld,
enthused by this human panorama, this rare unity of resolve.
Out of the blue, Josef climbed up on a hillock of soil and, with
his heart burning and his body swirling about like a living
flame, began to recite his own version of 'Brothers', a poem by
the great Yiddish poet I. L. Peretz, inspired in turn by Schiller's
ode, *To Joy*:

> *White and black and brown and yellow,*
> *Mix together all the colours —*
> *Jew or Pole or Turk or Arab,*
> *People everywhere are brothers!…*

But before long, on the first of September, German planes
darkened our skies. And a week later, a scaffold appeared in
Bałucki Rynek, our marketplace. Three men were hanging
from it, strung up as if to give us a taste of what we were in
for; they had white signs pinned to their lapels, bearing the
words *JUDE SCHWINDLER* scrawled in large black letters.
And as, to my dismay, I heard the tumultuous crowd argue
over the correctness of these executions, I knew that Isaiah's
utopia had been bitterly betrayed once more.

Moving away from the black spectacle, I bumped into my
friend Josef. His face was grey, and he seemed ten years older
than the last time I had seen him, three weeks earlier. And
Josef — who even after the catastrophe of these years would

not relinquish his belief in universal brotherhood; who never stopped repeating 'A *mensch* is a *mensch*', that all people are equal – Josef turned to me and said: 'All of this is just a temporary darkness that we'll overcome.'

No doubt he expected me to agree. After all, we were both Bundists, the idea of brotherhood was fundamental to our ideology. And he was still basking in that remarkable display of common endeavour of just a few weeks ago.

'My friend,' he continued without waiting for my response. 'Roses blossom only briefly, yet no one will deny their beauty.' And then, this incorrigible romantic added: 'One drop of radiant hope may help humanity cross over an ocean of despair.'

'That's all very well,' I told him as we parted, 'and it might even be true. But for the time being, Josef, we'd best observe the curfew…'

❧ The Sun in My Mother's Song ❧

Like most of my school friends I was brought up in a socialist spirit, in the belief that socialism would free our working-class parents from the drudgeries of life; that socialism – and, in the view of some of our people, Communism – would bring bread into our hungry homes. At the age of twelve, not one of us had yet read *Das Kapital*, Max Beer's *History of Socialism*, or other books dealing with that subject. Our educational literature consisted mainly of poetry and songs; every word in these songs and poems we took for gospel, since they spoke to us with an ingenious and trusting credibility. Mother had a beautiful voice, and after a day of hard work, in order to lull her wrenching pain to sleep, she loved to sing of the glory of the coming revolution.

I was quite convinced that the prophecies in my mother's songs would soon, very soon, be fulfilled. But history, like nature, is full of bizarre twists. So it was that on 23 August 1939 two mortal foes, Joachim von Ribbentrop and Vyacheslav Molotov, embraced each other in friendship, thereby making our time the victim of an abominable trick.

Shortly afterwards my sister Pola's friend, an ardent Stalinist, ran breathlessly into our flat. 'There are circumstances,' she shouted out of the blue at my father, whom she knew to be a confirmed anti-Communist, 'in which language cannot express the magnitude of a historic event... It's impossible,' she continued, her voice subsiding, 'to define the genius of Stalin's dialectic!'

My dad smiled hesitantly. Then, with a disconsolate gesture of refusal, he repeated the lines he had pencilled after the infamous Moscow trials:

From Warsaw to Paris,
From London to Iraq,
Has Moscow dispatched
Her bloody axe.

The woman stood there, an incredulous look on her face. 'Fascist!' she exclaimed, and brusquely walked out the door.

Nine days later, on 1 September 1939, as the dawn awoke from a nervous night dark with anticipation, and Molotov-Ribbentrop cocktails began to rain on our heads from the German bombers swarming overhead, I watched as the sun in my mother's song died on her lips.

✎ *Initiation* ✎

Friday morning, 8 September 1939, in the city of the waterless river. I happened to be standing on the corner of Lutomierska and Zgierska, facing the Church of St Mary and her tall, sad spires. The arms on the clock froze at a quarter to ten; they were not to budge for five years.

White flags of defeat fluttered obsequiously from every window, and high above, up in the unreachable sky, a solitary plane swam like a grey shark. Fear cannot always be seen, but one can be frightfully aware of its presence. In the foreboding stillness I picked up the poignant murmur of the cobblestones. For a split second I experienced the illusion that I was here alone, all alone; but before long, as if in a black-magic play, the street had come to life with throngs of blue-eyed, hefty-bosomed maidens carrying flowers in their naked arms, screaming *Heil! Heil! Heil!* at the oncoming invaders as they rolled through our town.

When I got home I found my father arguing with our religious neighbour, the widower Zilberszac. He was a tall, broad-shouldered man in his early sixties whose beard, pencilled with fine silvery strands that tumbled from his chin like a black waterfall, might have been the envy of the rabbinical world.

'No, Panie Gershon,' he was asserting, 'it won't be as bad as people are saying. Remember the Germans in the last war? Their incredible politeness, friendliness even, the business we used to do with them? Panie Gershon, my son the history teacher told me a remarkable thing. He told me that one should not forget Heinrich Grätz, who, after completing his *History of the Jews*, wrote to his grandfather that he had concluded the work with a joyful feeling — knowing, he said, that the Jews had at last not only found a just freedom in civilized lands, but had also gained a certain recognition.'

'Grätz was not the first or the last naive sage,' mother replied.

Mother's comment would come to seem like the prophecy of a Cassandra, because a week later, on the morning of the Sabbath, a distraught and bloodied Zilberszac, his face resembling a badly harvested field, fell into our room. The scene has hung in my memory like an exhibit suspended in a gallery that refused to close. My little mother, with wet towels, is bending over Zilberszac's bulky form; father runs to and fro with buckets of water; while the victim tries to explain what happened. 'I walked out through the gate quite early, the street was still sleeping... Out of the blue two young soldiers sprang at me... They forced me to kneel... One of them said, "I'm a master *Razierer*," and took out his pocket-knife!... I begged for mercy but he took no notice...'

All day long Zilberszac sat in our room like a silent tombstone in a forgotten cemetery. But as the evening wind began to blow out the waning daylight, and a grey cloud like a dishevelled witch appeared on our windowpane, he quietly stood up, walked to the door and, turning his face towards mother, said 'Thanks.'

Then, as if to himself, he added: 'Dusk is always the harbinger of night.'

❧ *Beginning* ❧

And the black magician said, 'Let there be darkness,' and there was darkness, and he saw that the darkness was good. And he separated the darkness from the light. He called the light night, and the darkness he called day. And there was morning and there was evening, the first day of his creation.

And on the second day he decreed that no Jew be allowed to walk on the footpath, or in the middle of the road. No Jew should be permitted to have a dog, cat, bird, money, gold, fur coat, piano, violin, mandolin, guitar, gramophone, or to breathe Aryan air. All Yiddish books and all writers who wrote in Yiddish were to be burned, their alphabet ground to dust, for one must not forget that it was a Jewish secret code, and that in each of its letters there dwelt a hidden flame that would destroy the holy darkness. One needed to watch the Jews closely, for they had an art of dreaming up dangerous schemes, their very presence and movements could modify the world.

And then he said, 'Let all the Jews be herded into one precinct,' and they were herded in, and he saw that the herding was good. And there was morning and there was evening, the third day of his genius.

At dusk, just past the curfew, we discussed our new situation. 'What is there to do?' someone asked. 'We are on a road that leads to no other roads.' Another replied, 'They may want to kill us, but we'll live through that as well. History is awash with butchers, yet we outlived them all.'

I listened to what father had to say — and would not have believed that this incurable doubter was able to utter such words. 'There is a certain freedom even in prison,' he declared, 'and we have to make the most of that.' Then he related a parable, which went something like this:

A prominent scientist once predicted the coming of a great catastrophe, a second flood that would destroy all humanity. The clergy, forever ideologically divided despite a common vested interest in the Almighty, quickly called an international conference. They advised each delegate to bring along his own God, in the hope that such a manifestation of religious fidelity might sway heaven to rescind so cruel a punishment. But as the members of the gathering were about to commence their deliberations, they were horrified to notice the absence of a single representative of the Jews. Messengers darted to and fro, but the tidings were gloomy: the Jews were not coming, and they remained unmoved. One emissary reported that, first of all, they were too busy studying how to live underwater. Secondly, they had been astonished to have been asked to bring their God — it had never occurred to them that one could carry ubiquity.

❧ *Snow in the Window* ❧

They were our neighbours for thirty years, yet we never knew their surname. There were no signs on our doors, and when the postman, like a town crier, called out from the yard the names on the letters he was delivering, our next-door neighbours were never among the recipients.

To remain an unknown entity in an open community such as ours — I mean within a tenement where people never locked their doors, where the women wandered openly in and out to pursue their daily rounds — creates perhaps a most vulnerable state of affairs for the family thus shielding itself. It opens the gates to fancy, to speculation and to endless tantalizing stories. But what I am about to relate (though most of it was told to me by my mother) belongs to a world of cruel and absurd realities.

The lady of the household was known to us as Zlata; her hunchbacked husband, an expert builder of ovens, was nicknamed 'The Mason'. He had been twenty-three when he married his thirteen-year-old Zlata, and although the young wife had played hopscotch while her Mason was at work, by the age of twenty she had borne him five healthy daughters.

The years sped by quickly, the girls grew up; before long they had left their teens behind. Unfortunately, none of them was married as yet. Zlata, by now well and truly up in arms, kept summoning the local matchmakers — including, in the end, the top man in the profession, the lame but learned Gavriel. Gavriel walked with a cane, was garbed in black from head to toe, wore a white straw hat on his head and, even at the height of summer, heavy galoshes on his feet.

'So,' Zlata asked him, 'how are you going to solve this problem?'

'Zlateniu,' pleaded the arch-matchmaker, 'life is but a dice throw. At the moment I have no one — especially for your twenty-year-old, flat-chested, anaemic-looking Sura. But give me time, and you'll soon reap the benefit of Gavriel's genius.'

And lo and behold, barely a fortnight later a first introduction took place between the hapless Sura and her prospective husband, the grey-haired and balding Matis Sznabel, an expert men's tailor. This was obviously the work of God. Matis was very fond of roast duck and baked apples, which turned out to be Sura's specialty, and it was love at first sight.

Mother recalled the tension that sunny midday — the nervous footsteps in our unlit corridor, the hasty shutting and opening of doors, the five sisters running into our room without asking our permission, dashing straight for the window, their excited shouts: 'They're coming! They're coming!… They're here!' They waited anxiously for a few more minutes; then all five of them, holding aloft five open black umbrellas (a status symbol in our district), marched back into their own apartment to greet Sura's future in-laws.

Matis proved to be a clever and industrious businessman — a good earner with bourgeois ambitions. After nine months Sura gave birth to a boy, whom they named Sevek. They moved out of our neighbourhood, to the part of town occu-

pied by the *nouveaux riches*. Sevek grew into a pleasant youngster, a good student, and a fine violinist with a love for the
German classics. We would see each other during his frequent
visits to his grandparents, and we became friends. Life was
good to Sevek. How could this gentle seventeen-year-old suspect the barbarism that lurked within the darkest folds of the
culture he worshipped.

All this by way of a background preamble.

On a snowy winter's morning in mid-January 1940, two
young men — dressed in black and in the company of the caretaker — entered the Sznabels' apartment and curtly ordered
them to vacate the premises and proceed to the newly proclaimed ghetto section of our town, where I still lived with my
family. The Sznabels quietly obeyed, but as they were about to
negotiate the staircase, the unwelcome visitors called Sevek
back. They told him to sit down, face the window and watch
the falling snow. For some minutes they amused themselves
by engaging him in useless conversation. Then, as one of
them was asking Sevek what he would like to do after the war,
the other unhurriedly took out his shiny revolver and put a
bullet through my friend's head.

For three days Sevek sat dead in his chair, his head covered
with a white sheet. Sura and Matis, having moved back to our
block, continued their life as best they could in the apartment
next door. Four years later, along with the rest of us, they were
deported to Auschwitz.

❧ *Kaddish for a Bantamweight* ❧

Adolek Kohn lived with his widowed mother, younger brother
Sholem, and a little white hen that answered to the name
Dolores. The four of them occupied a one-room ground-floor

apartment at Gnieźnieńska 10, where all the windows faced away from the sun. Adolek was always a great storyteller, but my favourite among all of his many ghetto tales is the one about the hen.

'You know, my friend,' he would begin, 'Ecclesiastes tells us that there is a season for everything, but in the ghetto there was only one season: death — death from hunger, from typhus, from tuberculosis, and death from diarrhoea. Well now, diarrhoea,' he had adopted a playful tone, 'is of course a feminine noun, and, like most creatures of the feminine persuasion, she, for some reason, found me attractive. No sooner had she taken me to bed than my snow-white Dolores, with her coquettish little red comb and her pert little neck, took to mooning about the room like a heartbroken ballerina.

'Meanwhile, Lady Diarrhoea, perhaps to spite Dolores, became almost despotic. Within one week she made me lose the use of my legs, numbed my fingers and froze my tongue. My eyes were still open, though mother was convinced I'd gone blind; but I could see her standing beside me, wringing her hands. The doctor she summoned gave me an injection, a sort of serum drawn from a dead horse which, unknown to the doctor, was infected with tuberculosis. It didn't cure me, but it actually saved me from contracting *that* horrible disease. However, as things went from bad to worse, mother implored God, my brother Sholem lit candles, and people started coming over; I heard their sing-song prayers for someone about to depart the world. At dusk my temperature would climb to dangerous heights. Dolores, in order not to see me expire, hid herself under my bed.

'One evening I heard a gentle rustle on the windowpane above my bed, as gentle as the touch of a lost kitten's paw. It was the angel of death. "Are you ready, Adolek Kohn?" he asked, not unpolitely, and not without a hint of irony. "Don't tarry, for I am very busy. It's peak season for departures in the ghetto."

'All at once, Dolores — not like a chook but more like a predatory eagle, her white plumage ruffled, her wings out-spread, her sharp beak greedy for combat — sprang from under my bed and swooped upon the intruder. That a hen can be aggressive and can fight is well known, but never had I witnessed such a feathery commotion. The angel of death must have decided I wasn't ready after all, for he seemed to have withdrawn. And next morning (I swear it), when my mother looked under the bed, Dolores stood up to reveal a fresh egg she'd been sitting on. She appeared to be saying: "Please, take it for your son, whom I love." The following morning there was another egg, and in the afternoon yet another. This went on for some days, and it was those eggs which put me back on my feet! I know it sounds unbelievable, but that's the way it was.

'After I recovered, Dolores followed me around like a puppy. If I sat down to read, she would make herself a little nest next to me. Once, when I touched her, I was sure there was a tear of gratitude in her button eye.

'Our next-door neighbour, an elderly gentleman, was con-vinced that Dolores was a *gilgul*, probably a *tzaddik* incarnate. When she passed away, he came to offer his profound con-dolences. "Adolek, you ought to say *Kaddish*," he solemnly advised me…'

Having finished his story, in a tone that always brought back the snow to my sunny window, my friend would sit back in his chair. 'What I have told you might give the impression that facts have been sacrificed to, shall we say, myth. Not at all. It's just that this incident was so wonderfully bizarre, and outside what we think of as "logical". So why, like a fool, do I keep telling and retelling it, over and over again? Not only because I took the advice of my wise old neighbour, that Dolores deserved *Kaddish*, but also to remind people that there were those who, although convinced that they had been created in God's image, did not even live up to the nobility of a little hen.'

◈ *A Song of Books* ◈

Books were the pride of a Jewish home. Seldom could a Jewish dwelling be found without at least a small library: *Tanach* (Bible) and Talmud, some prayer-books, and a few volumes of scriptural commentary. At the dawn of the twentieth century, our everyday spoken Yiddish was transformed by the flowering of a new literary Yiddish and this became the major cause of a mind-boggling harvest of books — books of wisdom, philosophy, poetry, history, art, science. Before long, the literary tongue had become the medium for hundreds and thousands of alluring translations of the Russian, French, German and English classics, opening the door, for the Yiddish reader, to a new sense of belonging, a whole new consciousness and sensibility.

On 12 February 1940 the skies swirled with grey clouds and white snow. At daybreak, from every corner of the city of the waterless river, came the Jews. They trudged obediently through terrain bleached white by the weather, trod behind little carts packed with their possessions, towards the ghetto that had been established for them by the Germans.

As I stood on the kerb observing the procession of mourners behind hearses bearing their own lives, I noticed a man on the opposite side. He seemed frozen to the spot. He had three small children and a woman beside him, her face a tapestry of murdered dreams. They stood defeated next to a broken-down cart. I offered my help, and together along the slippery cobbles we pushed their crippled wagon, tilting on one wheel and loaded with the family's past. And of course, there were books; many, many books.

Within an hour we were well-acquainted. Michael Rosz was in his late forties, tall, with brows so thick I could hardly make out his eyes. He was an educated man, an avid reader of both scripture and modern Yiddish literature. 'I was once a successful textile manufacturer,' he told me in a whisper so intense that he might have been imparting a state secret. 'We lived well, but what awaits us now only God can know.'

The road grew weary, our footfall heavy, and daylight longed for a rest. As we pushed the cart onwards I experienced something rather strange: I thought I could hear voices coming from among the books! The fatigue must have really got to me, for I was sure I could even hear them arguing and conversing together...

The Roszes were allotted a little hut in the yard of a tenement block. It was cramped and cold, and its roof was in need of repair, yet they were grateful. I helped them to unload their fine furniture, stacking some items on top of others, and left them to settle in. Over the months that followed I became a frequent visitor. On many an occasion I assisted Michael in chopping up the once-treasured pieces of his household to feed his sooty black stove.

The end of the year brought another sharp winter. The temperature fell to 18 below zero. Michael was bedridden, there was snow everywhere, but no bread and nothing left for the cold black monster, which hadn't been lit for weeks. Michael's desperate wife kept eyeing the books. 'Don't,' the sick man pleaded. 'Don't. A Jew who burns books might as well burn himself.'

'But some of them are damaged.'

'Books are living things,' Michael insisted. 'When they are injured they must be cared for. If they're beyond help, they have to be given a proper burial. Cremation is out of the question.'

Before long the Roszes received their 'wedding card', or resettlement notice. I went to say goodbye. Although Chaim Rumkowski, the ghetto Eldest, assured them that they would be better off where they were headed, Mrs Rosz wept bitterly. Overnight their hut had become a palace. But there was nothing they could do, their fate was sealed. As we embraced, Michael whispered, 'If you can, please take care of my books.'

I was never to see the Rosz family again.

A few days later, after dusk, I revisited their sad-looking hut. It seemed alive with an eerie emptiness. The books were strewn all over the dirty floor, some of them with pages torn out. I sat down amid the wreckage of my friend's precious library, and I must have dozed off, for I fell into a vivid dream.

Out of a battered volume of Sholem Aleichem, a heart-broken Tevye emerged. Throwing his arms apart, he shouted: 'We are burning, burning!... The flames!' At that moment I knew precisely what had happened to Michael, his wife and their three children.

I awoke with a jolt. It was almost midnight. 'Time to go,' I said to myself.

But as I touched the door, I imagined I could still hear Michael's torn-up Tevye, calling from the floor: *Take me with you, please, take my song. Sing it to those who don't see, sing it to those who won't know...*

☙ To Immortalize a Beggar ☙

Our neighbourhood was a fascinating gallery of characters, but if asked on whom I would bestow my first prize for sheer originality, I would choose the learned and pious beggar whom we called Shulem the Prince. Shulem was a rich man who became a pauper overnight. If you enquired how, he would respond, with an almost hidden grain of bitterness, that it was Satan's doing. 'And yet I am much better off than Job,' he would continue. 'I still have six hungry children at home, and a little wife standing next to her frozen stove, awaiting a miracle.'

Since he had no profession, Shulem took it upon himself to become a beggar. He quickly turned into the most respected beggar in our city. For one thing, he never begged on Mondays and Thursdays; on those two days, like most pious Jews, he fasted — because Monday was the day when Moses had ascended Sinai, and Thursday the day when he had come back down.

Since he was a particularly methodical man, Shulem's professional itineraries were well mapped out. He never visited the same home twice in the one week, and he knew exactly how much to expect from each household — so planning his expenditure was a breeze. The first twenty groshen he received he always put aside for *tzedakah* (charity), in aid of a school for disadvantaged boys. To Shulem, charity was of paramount importance in life. Without charity, he declared, the whole world would, God forbid, come to an end.

Well, it did. And as our homely thugs, on the orders of the ghetto authorities, and in the company of hundreds of other Jews, escorted his thirty-year-old wife and their six children (the oldest only nine) towards eternity, Shulem ran out from the crowd. 'God!' he screamed into the rooftops. 'Why?... Tell me why!'

Shulem immediately suffered a fit, collapsed, and died on the spot. Early next morning, a man who claimed to be a seer swore that he had heard, in the middle of the night, the voice of an embodied Tzedakah wailing, 'I am a widow, a widow, a widow!' Of course nobody believed him. But as the day showed itself, and the growing light revealed bizarre footprints on the otherwise untouched blanket of snow, our whole backyard fell under the spell of a deep and awesome foreboding.

❧ The Yellow Sniper ❧

Fatek was a born loser. He was a miserable-looking specimen, thin as a swamp reed, with insipid blue eyes and sloppy shoulders, a nose violet from drinking, cheeks as red as hot cinders, and a falsetto voice. His straw-coloured hair had earned him the nickname 'Yellow'.

Prior to the war, Fatek had spent most of his days in dimly-lit gaming joints, playing poker and assisting novices to master the art, in which he considered himself expert. At night Yellow would walk about on rubber-soled shoes, like any other noiseless 'locksmith'. Needless to say, his professional skills made him the local jail's favourite and most frequent guest.

His lucky break was the war. Not long after the steel helmets marched into our city of the waterless river, Yellow Fatek, in common with many of his hue, conveniently discovered that, at least on his mother's side, he was one of *them*. He was accepted as such, and was soon promoted to the role of helping to guard the Jews of the ghetto that had become our prison. Since he had often been arrested for stealing from these Jews, Fatek welcomed the opportunity to show them his brand of payback.

Stationed opposite 40 Zgierska Street — a huge grey building inhabited by dozens of families, and located not far from the footbridge which crossed that street — Fatek positioned himself strategically behind his red-and-white sentry box. From here the skilled thief could pick off his targets carefully, mainly young people who happened to lean out of windows, at

a self-imposed quota of six a day. After operating in this
fashion for a while, he was summoned to appear before his
superiors. Fatek was terrified; he was convinced that he would
be punished. 'Perhaps I overstepped the mark,' he thought.
But instead, to his pleasant surprise, he was rewarded (as
rumour had it) with a gilded medal and an increase in pay. 'Oh
my God,' he murmured to himself. 'What a wonderful war!'

To avoid being confronted with the brutal reality of a
childhood world that existed no more, I never went back to
revisit the wasteland our town became. Of Fatek's fate I
learnt much later, from an old neighbour I ran into on the
other side of the world. Once the war ended, this man told
me, Fatek had gone into hiding. He emerged towards the end
of 1945. One night, drunk and disconsolate, he was heard
screaming through his open window: 'Filthy Jews! First you
killed the Son of God, and then you killed my war!' Shortly
afterwards a single gunshot rang out — the last shot that
Yellow Fatek ever heard.

❧ *Yonas Lerer* ❧

If someone in our neighbourhood had enquired about Yonas
Lerer, he would have been met with a shrug of the shoulders
or a blank stare. But if that someone had asked even the
smallest child, 'Where can I find Yonas Shreiber?' the searcher
would immediately have been led to the man who, from his
boyhood, had established his home among the pages of the
Tanach.

Yonas Shreiber ('Scribe'), an honoured disciple of the Alexan-
derer Rebbe, Isaac Menachem (who was gassed in Treblinka in
1943), had a white ghostlike face decorated with a pair of curly

pitch-black sidelocks. He was always dressed in a black silk frock-coat and, in accordance with tradition, tied a braided cord around his waist, to divide the upper spiritual part of his body from its lower profane counterpart. Like most devotees, he wore his black trousers tucked into white woollen socks.

Yonas was blessed with a wife and seven sons.

In his free time — that is, when he was not studying — he walked about the streets exhorting people, Jews and Gentiles alike, to be virtuous. 'Please, please,' he would urge, 'for your own and our world's sake, do good deeds, and keep your tongue from speaking evil.' At the start of our ghetto life, Yonas was a ray of hope; he saw God's hand in everything. 'Don't despair,' he pleaded with his fellow Jews. 'It is all from Him! Bless your troubles, praise the Almighty, and you will hasten the coming of the Messiah.'

But when our enemies did to him what the Babylonians had done to Zedekiah, the last king of Judah — forced Yonas to witness the murder of his sons, having bludgeoned him with the butt-ends of their rifles for asking to be killed first — he became totally disillusioned with his Master's goodness and wisdom. He abandoned the pages of his once-adored scriptures, stopped speaking to people, and went about his slaughtered world with a cadaverous look in his eyes.

One night, while reciting a tearful *Kaddish* after his sons, he glanced up and saw the obscene grin of a solitary cloud. He felt a light touch on his shoulder. It was Madness, quietly entering the darkened chambers of Yonas's heart.

God, it told him, *has passed on to you your father's and your father's fathers' misfortunes, a holy inheritance. And so it should be, from father to son, from son to son. To be chosen remains your destiny; it is attested by your children being put to death.*

'So what am I to do?' asked Yonas Lerer. 'How am I to live now?'

You are a fortunate man, Madness replied. *You have three choices — not everyone is given three choices.*

'What are these three choices?'

The first, my friend, is to forget everything, and exist like a lantern without a light. The second is to remember everything, and convert your heart into a graveyard.

'And the third?'

The third is, in my opinion, the best of all. Bind the first two choices into one, and walk for the rest of your days like me, in the guise of a man.

∾ *Pantomime* ∾

Frederick the Great, enlightened ruler of Prussia and a disciple of Voltaire, confronts his costly clergy. 'If you won't show me proof that there is a God,' he says, 'no more money will be forthcoming into your already fat coffers.' One of the churchmen steps forward. 'The Jews!' he exclaims. 'Look at everything we've done to them through the ages, and yet they're still around. That, surely, is unequivocal evidence that there is a God.'

Well, some two centuries later, the madman to the west who controlled our world — and who, at moments of violent exultation, believed there was nothing in all creation as splendid as himself — decided, with the acquiescence (for the time being) of his ephemeral partner to the east, to prove the cleric wrong.

The first step was the old device of declaring the potential victim to be vermin, a premise which most of his followers enthusiastically embraced — for it is much easier to squash a bug than another man. The next was to have the victims concentrated in one spot, so that extermination might proceed in an orderly manner. Order, of course, was very much at the heart of the madman's design. None the less, to furnish the process of 'in-gathering' with especial zest, he went out of his way to invert God's system. *Let there be chaos!* he shrilled, and there was chaos. On 7 and 8 March 1940, in our city of the waterless river, a horde of his savage heroes embarked on a murderous spree which cost hundreds of Jews their lives. On 1 May the ghetto was sealed off.

One evening, as mother placed our 'dinner' before each of us — a steaming dish of water where a lonely potato struggled in vain to avoid its fate — father remarked, mostly to himself: 'One tries to get to the bottom of things, but it's all just a running around in circles. History is absurd, events escape the control of reason. Time to withdraw into our own little world if we can.'

Shortly afterwards Ruven Rosen, a pious friend of ours with a glass eye (a memento of his fight for Polish independence in 1918), paid us a visit. He was barely recognizable. The Germans had ripped off his beard with a kitchen knife — the same indignity suffered the previous year by our neighbour Zilberszac, and an increasingly common occurrence in the streets of our town. Ruven was in dire need of consoling, for he sought some confirmation that what was happening was God's will. Father refused to accommodate such a notion. 'A God who is not a good God,' he declared, 'is no God at all. If He created man in His own image, why did we turn out so utterly debased?'

As if from a house on fire, Rosen ran out of our room, heartbroken. 'Blasphemer!' he screamed as he went. 'Desecrator!' Father dashed out after him and, full of remorse, escorted him back. 'Reb Rosen, please,' he pleaded. 'I didn't mean to offend you. I'm just bitter, like any other Jew these days. But if God willed this, then I cannot and will not forgive.'

Our neighbour fell into an inconsolable stupor. I inspected him out of the corner of my eye. He was clearly in pain, but it also struck me that without his beard he resembled a featherless chook. Father's razor gaze froze my smile.

That night a gang of thugs torched our synagogue.

❧ *Puppet State* ❧

A mad state in a mad world, hemmed in between timber boards and barbed wire, like a chicken-coop, and guarded by killers. Though it behoves me to say, that while one might still outwit the latter abominations, one could never conquer the unnavigable sea of hate which the local populace had so deftly dug out around us.

Little Shmulik, our local jester, who while still a boy would be sent to meet his Maker, once asked my father — whom everybody in our yard except myself considered a sage — why his former school friend Jurek, who lived across the fence, refused to respond to his greetings. 'Well,' father told him, 'he wants to be an exemplary member of his stock, so he must above all demonstrate his hatred for Jews; anything less would be suspect.' I don't know whether Shmulik understood this answer, but he nevertheless thanked my dad and walked off.

For those of us inside the fence, understanding had come quickly enough. The appointed Jewish 'king' of the ghetto, our puppeteer, was Chaim Rumkowski. Industrious, cunning, alert, a man with an arresting appearance who in other times might have been certified for the things he said and did, he could definitely not be regarded as a disappointment to his bosses. For not only did he successfully establish the order desired by his masters in the city of the waterless river; in the process, and much to the liking of his illustrious superiors, he ingeniously mimicked their own state. Chaim even resorted to their own obscene didacticism in embracing the proposition that orderly removal of unproductive elements was conducive to the future of our communal life.

From the very inception of the Jewish ghetto police, his commissars, sergeants and privates, even his fire-brigade, wore special uniforms complete with polished jackboots that imitated the Germans' terrible footfall. To deepen the dichotomy between themselves and the ordinary ghetto Jew, these scoundrels, mostly former high-school students, would not speak Yiddish but only the Polish tongue. Consequently they considered themselves not just a people apart, but the true aristocracy of Chaim's cobweb empire — and with good reason. They and their families were generally exempted from the expulsions from their homes; moreover, they lived well, never going hungry in a city that was starving, going instead on recreation leave within the enclave that was our twilight zone.

On one occasion, during an official function for the privileged ghetto elite, as the night reached its intoxicating climax, the regal Chaim — around his neck a silver chain bearing a Star of David — called out to his festive gathering: 'Gentlemen, I am bound to share with you some important news. The war will soon come to an end, but let me assure you: the Ghetto will continue as before. Of course, at the rate we're going now,' he added, 'there will be a shortage of workers, and as you know, work is our golden passport to life. But I've been told that new Jews will be brought in, Jews from all the corners of Europe. And I, my dear friends, with God's help, will continue to take care of all the citizens of the ghetto, and to protect you all, as I have always done…'

The only defence of the average ghetto-dweller against Chaim and his henchmen's vulgarity, the one defence of the starving impoverished workers who spat out their lungs over the sewing or textile machines or in the carpentry workshops, was the sarcastic verses and aphorisms which the poet's lacerated heart sang into posterity.

Behind the wires, by cosy fires,
The scum are singing, united in crime:
'Let's drink L'Chaim to our sovereign Chaim,
To juicy roast and a red French wine.'

As daylight betrayed the day, and dusk squeezed its grey smirk against the pane of our workroom, Efraim the Chassid (so called because of his deep religiosity), presser in our tailoring unit, would shake his head. 'My God, how is it that our common fate has not transcended our differences?' And then, paraphrasing the opening lines of the Lamentations, he would chant:

How lonely sits the city
of the waterless river.
She that was once great with people
has become like a widow.
She that was a princess among the cities
has become a vassal.
Bitterly we weep in the night…

∾ Missed Curfew ∾

I got home almost an hour past curfew. Mother was trembling with fear. Father, although engaged in a discussion with our good friend, the ever-starving Mechel Schiff, fixed me with a questioning gaze. I wanted to explain my lateness, but our guest wouldn't give me a chance: he was an excellent talker, a terrific dialectician, and he was running hot.

'Language is the physical manifestation of man's spirituality,' he declared, raising his voice slightly.

'I agree,' answered father, forgetting my indiscretion for the moment. 'But I am curious as to how you arrive at such a fine postulate.'

Apart from his erudition in philosophy, Mechel was a poet at heart. 'A mundane explanation may pose some difficulties,' he suggested, after a considerable delay. 'It's hard to articulate because it is buried in one's subconscious, hidden in the crevices between spoken words.'

How they could debate metaphysical propositions on an empty stomach was beyond me.

'My dear Mechel,' said my father, 'I'm afraid this is all a bit above my head.' I detected a hint of irony in his voice.

'Is that my fault?' said Mechel.

Mother placed before him a dish of hot floury liquid and a slice of bread. Our visitor was overwhelmed with gratitude. The steam rising from this feast masked his tears as he ate — with vigour and a good deal of noise. Finally, wiping his mouth with his dirty handkerchief, he turned his attention to me.

'And so tell us, young man, what detained you for so long? Was it worth risking your life for?'

We had never had any secrets from Mechel — he was one of us. 'I attended a meeting of our underground cell,' I said at once. 'Our cell leader, Bono, spoke about the hunger in the ghetto, the deaths. We decided to compile a list of all those who have now conveniently discovered that they're *Volksdeutsch*.'

Mechel stood up in his seat. 'There won't be any retributions!' he cried. 'Jews are not a vindictive people. Get it out of your hot heads, it goes against our psyche—'

'What *is* our psyche?' I cut in.

'A spirit born of a marriage between exile and promise. An ethos born of an eternal Exodus. Jews quickly forgive and forget — little wonder that the Bible repeats the word *Remember* a hundred and sixty-nine times. Obviously our scribes knew us well.'

At this point father spoke up, doubtless to interrupt Schiff's homily. 'So tell me, friend,' he said, holding up his open palm. 'Your home is but a shed, you have no wife, no children, not even a relative to speak of. Why didn't you escape like many of the others — like our heroic government did before the Germans invaded our city?'

Mechel grew suddenly tense, pensive, framing his response. At last he announced:

'A city can survive without a king, but not without a fool.'

The light outside had grown dim. We had known that the evening was coming, but now that it had arrived we were thrown off-balance, almost shocked. 'You can't risk going back at this hour,' mother told our guest, 'I won't let you. It's far too late.'

'What's more, the yellow sentry is on night duty,' my father added. 'You must stay.'

Mechel stayed, and left at daybreak. We never saw him again.

❧ *Those Incredible Believers* ❧

The city of the waterless river was renowned for its colourful working class, its many political parties and factions, its stormy May Day demonstrations, and the socialist fervour that so passionately guided the Jewish working community in its unshakeable belief that it was an integral part of the one great universal fraternity.

My neighbourhood had good reason to be proud. Though famous for its poverty, it was inhabited by hundreds of gifted artists, singers, musicians and thinkers who had never had the chance to display their skills, along with scores of religious and secular messianic redeemers. I lived in the heart of an iridescent kaleidoscope, a veritable bazaar of diverse people and ideas — the kind of place you would expect to experience only in a storybook. A local wit put it another way: out of the nine thousand denizens of our precinct, at least ten thousand were poets!

Back in 1934, the socialist uprising in Austria and the Schutzbund's heroic stand against the Fascist forces had converted my street into a raging ocean. From daybreak, crowds gathered around newspaper stands; men forgot their starving families, downed their tools, talked only of joining the bloody fray. As a rain of coins drummed into the tin fundraising dish, Sam Samionov, the local baritone, had clambered on the shoulders of two burly revolutionaries and, in concert with the whole swaying, rhapsodizing clamour, burst into the inspirational song of the moment:

O lead us, flaming red flags —
into a new dawn we stream;
towards those men and women,
our fighting comrades of Wien...

To our great dismay, a few years later some of our Viennese comrades, the very ones for whom we had been ready to lay down our lives, would volunteer to become guards patrolling the ghetto perimeter — to reassure themselves that none of their Jewish friends would escape its fate. Yet even then, our ghetto Bundists, those incredible believers, continued to commemorate Lassalle, Sacco, Vanzetti, the fall of the Bastille — while the French did their dirty work in Drancy. May Day, the day of hope, of international brotherhood, retained a special place in the hearts of these starving, betrayed Jewish workers, and despite repeated setbacks and adversities they never failed to uphold its significance.

By this time I was employed as a machinist in a clothing factory at 13 Żabia Street, which had once housed a primary school. The building was situated almost directly across from the border with the forbidden outside world. My unit consisted of twenty men (tailors) and three women (finishers). May Day had to be celebrated in great secrecy, since our factory commissar, a man in his mid-twenties and an officer in the Jewish police — with a face resembling an elderly sheep and the voice of a young rooster — was a noted squealer. On the festive day, we arrived at the entrance earlier than ever. I was greeted by my daring friend, Blumenfeld, our oldest and most respected tradesman. He presented me with a piece of red thread, to be wound around the little finger, and before we knew it someone had coined the idea of a 'Day of the Red Threads' — a day of tension, sabotage and revolt.

In the course of the working day, however, our rebellious mood fizzled out. We left work at dusk. Walking out the gate, we were immediately confronted by the border fence, and beyond it the other side of life. I happened to look up. Through the dusty pane of a lit window, a carefree little girl was waving sweetly to us. Perhaps it was this that, without warning, provoked one of the younger members of our team to brave the treacherous silence:

So comrades, come rally
And the last fight let us face;
The Internationale
Unites the human race...

Abruptly, someone grabbed the child from behind and quickly doused the light, and darkness shrouded the dusty window once more.

❧ *Anna* ❧

We met in 1940, in the late autumn, at night, on a narrow unlit winding staircase. The stairs were not wide enough for two, so we had to struggle to squeeze past. Although we could hardly see each other's face, the momentary contact between our bodies was electrifying, and the repetition of the experience — which became decreasingly 'accidental' — eventually brought us together. Before coming to the ghetto, Anna had been a mathematics teacher at a high school. At thirty, she was twelve years my senior, and married, but her husband was missing in the war. 'I live by myself,' she told me. 'It's not easy.' And so, after several more staircase encounters, most of which I cunningly arranged, she invited me to her room.

'What do you do with yourself,' she asked me, 'on these long and tedious ghetto nights?' Anna was a plain-spoken, strong-headed woman, physically and intellectually superior to me, not to mention a head taller. Her hair was a dark shade of blond, and she had deeply-set eyes, blood-red lips, and whitish skin which firmly enveloped a nimble figure. She was beautiful, if not particularly pretty.

'When there's peace,' I replied, meaning the times between murder and murder when we hallucinated respite, 'I read and write.'

'Are you a writer?'

'I hope to be.'

'And what do you write about?'

'Life, people, love and hate.'

'Would you write a story about me?' She raised a mischievous eyebrow.

'Certainly…'

'You know that most writers long to go to bed with their
heroines, if only in their imagination. But nothing can replace
the real thing — it's an act that reveals one's true character.'

What a great opening for a story, I thought.

A story opening wasn't the only thing on my mind.

The next evening I went straight from work to Anna's
room. I had the impression that she had been expecting me,
though she seemed unusually nervous. Turning away, she
began to unbutton her white cotton blouse. I watched mesmerized as her little breasts played hide-and-seek. A moment
later she let her navy-blue skirt fall to the floor. She wore no
underpants. I stared at her snow-white buttocks, and, when
she finally turned towards me, at her long red nipples,
which seemed disproportionately large for her small thinly-
veined breasts. My body and my mind were on fire, my blood
was pounding. I tore off my own clothes, and before I knew
it the thing was done. Anna was visibly disappointed, even
angry.

'You express yourself so fluently when we speak,' she
remarked, not without sarcasm, 'yet in the language of sex
you're still a beginner.'

I tried to apologize.

'Don't,' she said. 'Lovemaking is not about being apolo-
getic, but more about being… apocalyptic. Union between a
man and a woman embraces the whole universe. Each encounter is a new act of destructive restoration.'

I was growing extremely uneasy; in fact, I was sinking into
a deep distress. What was worse, Anna felt sorry for me. She
was clearly looking for a way to revoke what, just minutes
before, had appeared so irrevocable.

Then I heard her redeeming whisper. 'It's not entirely your fault,' she was telling me. 'I underestimated your fierce spontaneity — that is something a woman should never do. I promise you, next time it will be better.'

And so it was. And after a few weeks of diligent practice we achieved what I thought must be the highest level of carnal harmony.

It was too good to last. Because the day came when I knocked on Anna's door and, to my horror, was answered by a man's gruff voice. 'Who's there?' it demanded.

I was shattered. Like a thief I sneaked away on tiptoe. Hoping desperately that she wasn't home from work yet, I waited near the foot of the stairs for Anna's return.

She greeted me with a strange smile. 'My husband came back,' she said.

It was as I had feared. 'So… what about us?' I muttered.

'*Us*? Don't even dare to ask.'

'You're cruel Anna, very cruel,' I heard myself tell her.

'So is life,' she snapped, and coldly squeezed past, abandoning me on the narrow bottom landing of our dark and winding staircase.

❧ *Across the Wire* ❧

My school friend and party comrade Sol Lichtensztajn, carried away by the tide of events, was forever in the thick of things. He lived with his mother, his one-legged father and his two little sisters in a one-room apartment on Dolna Street; in pre-ghetto days his parents had owned a tobacconist's kiosk nearby. Sol's father had excelled himself in the 1920 battle known in Polish history as *Cud nad Wisłą* (Miracle on the Vistula), where he lost his right leg and, for his bravery, was rewarded with a licence to sell cigarettes, an activity over which the government held a monopoly.

The war brought severe hunger to the Lichtensztajn household. In no time, tuberculosis took care of one of Sol's sisters, a suspicious cough confined his mother to bed, and the day-long nervous *thud-thud* of his father's wooden leg drove my friend to the brink. Sol had jesting blue eyes, a thick blond mane over his forehead, and a strong wiry body; he resembled a Polish country lad far more than a city-dwelling Jew.

At the end of September 1940, early on a crisp Sunday morning when God was still resting, Sol crept quietly out of his home, determined to procure some food for his dying mother. He walked up and down Dolna Street, and when he thought the sentry on guard duty was looking the other way, he leapt with the swiftness of a cheetah across the barbed-wire fence that separated this part of the ghetto from the rest of the city. But he wasn't quite swift enough, for as he leapt he was struck by a bullet from the rifle of the *Schupo*, as members of the Schutzpolizei, the German police, were known. His body was left dangling across the fence-wire.

When my underground circle met, towards dusk that day, we greeted each other with great sadness. It was not that we weren't accustomed to death — after all, the killing of Jews had become a daily occurrence. But we thought of ourselves as family, and it's different when one of your own is murdered. For a good while we sat together in silence. Then, because we knew that the deed had been committed by a young Austrian, who before the war might easily have been a fellow socialist, we began to recall the 1934 uprising in Vienna, and some names of leaders that were dear to us: men such as Koloman Wallisch, Julius Deutsch, and of course Franz Munichreiter, chief of the fire-brigade, whom, because of a stomach wound he sustained in the failed rebellion, the Fascists brought to the gallows on a stretcher…

'How passionately we were involved in their fight,' one of us remarked, 'sending our meagre earnings to help the starving children of Karl Marx Hof.'

'It wasn't just *their* fight, but also ours,' Bono, our cell leader, reminded us. 'And it still is. This war was not started by our comrades but by a madman, a megalomaniac who craves immortality. Well, his end will come, I can assure you.' He nodded his head portentously, staring into the distance.

'According to an ancient legend,' he resumed a few moments later, 'there was once a holy temple in Athens, constructed of light, hope and peace. One night, a deranged, talentless man who hungered after renown set the temple aflame; when it lay in ashes he ran into the marketplace and, to the astonishment of its peaceful citizens, screamed, "I put the temple to the torch! I put the temple to the torch!" For this, the sages of Athens proclaimed a heavy punishment: that no one should ever speak to the malefactor, no one should offer him shelter, no one should provide him with food; and that upon his death he should be left in the gutter to rot, until his corpse would turn the stomachs of vultures... Today, the same fate awaits that infamous arsonist in Berlin!'

I think Sol's was the last party interment in the ghetto. About twenty of us, bareheaded in the late-afternoon breeze, stood around the grave. Someone threw a red handkerchief into the open pit, and as the soil was tossed in and the makeshift coffin of our dear murdered comrade was covered by a sad and growing mound of fresh earth, Bono uttered a few valedictory words. Then, to the rhythm of the not-too-distant steps of the guard patrolling nearby, we began to murmur a familiar tune:

There is no might that can bar our way
or hinder with fear our hands;

we will transform into sunshine the night
with workers of all other lands…

The day took on a nondescript greyness. At curfew we dispersed, cautious as shadows. Our mood was sombre, yet somehow the incandescent light that our parents, our school and our party had implanted within us, the light we believed capable of transforming night into sunshine, helped us now. It would continue to guide us through a world grown so utterly forlorn.

≈ *The Chosen* ≈

One can be wise and yet quite naive; one can be stupid yet extremely cunning. I would say that Schicklgruber, our nemesis to the west, was rather the latter. Like his partner Dzhugashvili in the east, he had the craftiness to pick, from among thousands, the right man for the right job. Armed with the knowledge of exactly what credentials they were after, his thugs began their search for a suitable servant-tyrant. Chaim Rumkowski happened to be in the right place at the right time. His face was beaming with acceptance. He didn't realize what he was taking on…

('Who am I that I should go to Pharaoh?' pleaded Moses, God's lawgiver. 'I am not a man of words.' Nonentities, on the other hand, are forever eager to rule.)

Chaim — a man in his mid-sixties, uneducated, with restless eyes and a questionable past, grey-headed like a Greek philosopher and imbued with Herodian dreams — proved the perfect choice. Initially he had a council of thirty-one to help him execute the master regime's agenda. But on 7 November 1940, all but two of them were murdered. Meanwhile, up to 168,000 Jews were crammed into an area of just over four square kilometres, among them numerous people with small children, or with sick or lame parents. Some were desperate for shelter but shelter was hard to come by; we were among the lucky ones, old legitimate citizens of the squalor known as Bałuty, where the inverted state was set up.

Jews are forever carrying on a love-affair with hope — if there were an Olympiad of hoping, my people would invariably take out all the gold. Consequently we quickly became accustomed to our permanently ephemeral existence.

To show his Top Dog that he was worthy of the paper crown, Chaim the puppeteer established, almost overnight, a viable industry that churned out the finest product. For this our little Machiavelli was paid in food, which he distributed primarily amongst his chosen associates, along with their families and friends.

As hunger continued to whittle away at the ghetto population, and the cemetery blossomed with unburied corpses, and people had to enter in the middle of the night to locate and identify their dear ones, a storm of discontent shook Chaim's town. On 24 August 1940 a broadsheet appeared on ghetto walls:

*All the starving throughout the Ghetto will assemble on
Sunday, August 25, at 9.00 a.m., at 13 Lutomierska Street.*

Brothers and Sisters!

*Let us turn out en masse to eradicate once and for all, in
unison and by concerted force, the terrible poverty and the
barbarian conduct of community representatives toward the
miserable, exhausted, famished populace. Let every man do
his humane duty to his kin and carry the cry:*

Bread for All!

Enlist in the war against the accursed community parasite.
We demand that soup kitchens be opened in the blocks.

Next morning, Lutomierska Street was awash with vexa-
tion. Speaker after speaker incited the starving multitude to
revolt. Suddenly, amid the turbulent throng, my dear friend
Shmulik emerged from the crowd and, without hesitation,
hopped on the roof of a nearby shed and sang a ditty composed
on the spot:

Our Chairman Chaim
is an old mad hatter,
Ghetto Jews are starving,
he grows fatter and fatter.

When all these tidings reached Chaim, he was furious. 'Is
this what I get for sacrificing my whole life for them?' he
screamed. Swiftly he summoned his leader's henchmen. After
all, law and order was under serious threat. They came, fired
their rifles into the air, and went. That night, over a roast
duck for supper, Chaim grumbled: 'My whole ghetto is at
stake, my dreams, and all they can think of is bread!'

≈ *Herman Hecht* ≈

On a bright morning in the autumn of 1941, a black limousine
whose occupants included two uniformed members of the
Gestapo drove into our street. Without a word, they handed
over to the Sonderkommando, the special unit of the Jewish
ghetto police, a large, tall, outlandish-looking man dressed in
a navy-blue suit, white shirt, red tie with matching breast-
pocket kerchief, and polished black shoes. In his right hand he

carried a brown leather suitcase of a kind never seen in our neighbourhood, and across his left arm was draped a beige-coloured trenchcoat.

Our first meeting took place when the new arrival, plagued by a nagging hunger (to which we seasoned ghetto-dwellers were quite accustomed), asked for advice about how to exchange his trenchcoat for bread. He found it difficult to fathom the pushy locals, their skill at queuing up for food, their corrupted German tongue, their unrelenting Sisyphean struggle for life. When I tried to explain to Herman, who was twice my age, a few facts about ghetto life and ghetto people, he cut me short. 'There is nothing to defend,' he said. Well, there was; but he — the once debonair gentleman, with an air suited to his former standing in society, forced unexpectedly to dwell in a dim room with a leaky roof, who hung about the public kitchens or walked around like a lunatic, in vain search-ing the gutters for a forgotten potato-peel — he could not or would not understand.

About a year later, the black limousine once again drove into our street, picked up a resigned, sallow-faced Herman without ceremony, and drove off. This event coincided with the ongoing process of 'resettlement', so we assumed that the proud citizen of the great capital to the west would go the way all Jews were condemned to go. But to my pleasant surprise, just days later Herman was chauffeured back into our street. That evening I found him weeping on his bed. He was delirious — perhaps he thought he was dying. After a while he settled down, his Germanic Yiddish grew clearer; as I listened, a picture of the man's past was coming to life.

'I was born in 1900, into wealth,' he began. 'My father, a respected international merchant, decorated with the Iron Cross for his valour during the Great War, was a man of great benevolence and built many hospitals all over Germany. My mother was a well-known doctor. We lived in a palace, I was sent to the best schools, our library was one of the finest in Berlin, I loved reading and writing. We considered ourselves Germans, without asking our neighbours what *they* thought of us. At the age of twenty-two I married the most beautiful Aryan woman in the land; my two daughters — born, in accordance with my wife's wishes, in Spain — are fine young ladies, they haven't stopped lobbying for my release from this place. They are all so beautiful, so amazingly beautiful,' and he pulled out a tattered photograph. 'No, my loyal wife hasn't forgotten her husband, nor my children their father; last month they saw the Spanish ambassador — after all, my daughters were born in Spain, so an audience was granted. But when they saw me, my dear wife fainted and the girls couldn't stop howling. They kissed the boots of the guards to let me go. The guards told them, "You're behaving like Jews!" but they couldn't stop crying, my heart was shattered into little pieces. No, friend, I don't want to live, not any more. It's all so stupid,' he whispered, 'so incredibly stupid.'

The following morning a strange quiet hung about Herman's room, almost a frozen hollowness. I feared the worst, and I was right. As I came closer, I noticed a slip of paper with my name on it. 'Friend,' the note read, 'if you survive, please tell my story.' And below that simple message, a few more lines scrawled in a shaky German hand:

I lived in many worlds
Few of them my own,
Everywhere in exile
Everywhere alone.

❧ *Lipek's Irony* ❧

Lipman Biderman, whom his friends called Lipek, was a remarkable young man. I had known him from childhood. We had gone to the same kindergarten, often shared a desk at school, belonged to the same youth movement, read the same books. There were no secrets between us, and much of our free time we spent in each other's company.

Lipek was a well-built youngster with straight shoulders, a pitch-black mane that topped an elongated face, and a few freckles around his shapely nose. Two dark rings under his lower lids emphasized the slightly melancholic look in his stark black eyes.

There was a rare harmony between Lipek's mind and tongue, and he had an extraordinary way of expressing himself. His favourite mode was irony. Irony, he would explain, has many faces; you have to pick the one that fits you best, otherwise you'll appear a caricature. Lipek was regarded as a paragon of discourse among his peers, and I can't recall him ever pressing an argument that didn't make sense.

Once, in a political discussion just before the beginning of the war, I had heard him remark: 'Time is both eternal and ephemeral; one has to be an inventor to use it prudently.' And he continued: 'Time has its own furtive agenda — more than once in our history it has surprised not only its denizens but its very self.' One of the group couldn't resist wondering out loud: 'And what locality, sir, has the honour of claiming *you* as a denizen?' 'Paradise,' the answer rang out (Lipek was just sixteen); 'I dare say there is no substitute for the inevitable.' He didn't know how prophetic that answer was.

As the vulgar vortex took full control of our lives, and our world of speculative illusion was replaced overnight by bitter reality, I revisited my friend, by now confined to his bed. We'd not seen each other for some time. He had a dry, hoarse cough and there were beads of sweat on his forehead. 'At sunset my temperature rises,' he said. 'To keep me warm, of course.' Noticing that I had spotted a copy of Thomas Mann's *The Magic Mountain* by his bedside, he observed: 'You've no doubt read it — the Mountain of the Dying, where life's glee is a waning ember and where all dreams end in fever. I hope one day to be there, to sit like Hans Castorp in the subtle shadows, inhaling the wisdom of the Renaissance man Settembrini, and then to lie with a smile between the breasts of the beautiful Clavdia. Do you know how often I've imagined Clavdia's budding virtues…?'

But it was not to be. One winter evening, as my friend's temperature rose, two uniformed men entered Lipek's apartment. His mother pleaded with them to let her son remain at home. They dragged him out of bed and handed him over to the thugs to whom they swore allegiance. At the break of dawn, while the gods were still snoring under their sky-blue eiderdowns, Lipek, renowned paragon of our youth, was marched off to a desolate place and shot.

≫ *Promise* ≪

Nisek Golusz, known for his infectious laugh and effervescent personality, had been the most promising student in our school, a favourite with teachers as well as classmates. An exceptionally well-read teenager, by fourteen he was already at home with the French and Russian classics, and according to all predictions was a future professor of literature.

At school we were never very close: maybe because we belonged to two different economic strata, or perhaps because he lived in what was essentially a non-Jewish district — but more than anything because his intellectual horizons were so much wider than mine.

Even as children, the gulf in our awareness of the world had been immense. I still recall the freezing winter's morning in January 1933, when ten-year-old Nisek arrived at school with tidings whose seriousness none of us youngsters understood. 'Germany,' he had announced, his voice grave with foreboding, 'has elected a new Chancellor.'

Yet as the little Austrian usurped ubiquity, as his creepers entangled our walls in the high season of the absurd, while cut-throats in unlit corners lay in wait and searchlights kept morality at bay, our friendship blossomed and we began to spend time together. Once, as we walked arm in arm with our heads bare on the holy Sabbath, a passing religious Jew called out, 'Scum!' Nisek turned to the man and fired back, 'To insult your fellows is to insult God.'

By then I had become a part of his circle. We were a group of seven: six boys and a girl. A weaponless unit in the unarmed underground, we called ourselves the Flying Brigade and we dreamt of an uprising. We would meet every second week to discuss the political situation and the state of the war. Nisek, who carried on a perpetual love-affair with life, knew the atlas by heart and always had something positive and encouraging to say about the action on the various fronts. He would not be defeated by Rommel's successes in North Africa, and enthusiastically invoked the spirit of the great Russian commander Kutuzov.

Nine years after he had brought his ominous news to school, the Führer's thugs informed Nisek and his family that they had been selected for resettlement (at that time none of us knew the sinister meaning of that term). We all turned up to say goodbye, never doubting our dear friend's return. A few weeks later his coat came back — in its breast pocket a bullet-pierced, blood-smirched memento: Nisek's old school certificate, neatly folded and full of promise.

❦ My Uncle's Jacket ❦

Father's older brother Avraham was a happy soul, and an extremely lucky entrepreneur. In 1903 he had successfully established a textile factory — in his dining-room! — and he never looked back. He had two huge wooden hand-weaving machines, and worked on one of them for sixteen hours a day. On the other machine was a young newly-wedded man from just outside town, whose way of life kept the sun locked out of his face. Since work began at daybreak and finished late at night, he could see his new wife only on the Sabbath.

Unlike my father, Uncle Avraham wore the traditional Jewish garb, prayed to God every morning, kept the commandments, and wouldn't hear of politics. His aim in life was a good meal and a sound business. And yes, he did well, very well. In fact the constant visits to the butcher by his wife, my buxom aunt Chaya, an expert in the culinary arts, used to create an envious wagging of tongues in our neighbourhood.

Avraham was a granary of stories, and his specialty was the fable. I remember him telling me on one visit: 'When God created our world, He also created a speck of air and a speck of dust.' 'Uncle,' I interrupted, 'what is a speck of air?' He smiled at this. 'Please, young man, a fable does not need a parable. Anyway, the speck of air,' he resumed, 'floated around joyously, and still floats around today, without complaint. But the speck of dust always collides with somebody's eye. And who do you think suffers the most, the dust or the eye?' I shrugged. 'Both suffer!' announced my uncle triumphantly. 'The eye, because of the speck; and the dust, because it loses its freedom!'

But soon enough, war and the ghetto destroyed Avraham's happiness. The four sons and two daughters he had fathered in the alcove where he slept with his wife went off or were sent away, and never came back. In the end the only consolation from his once-flourishing textile enterprise was his two wooden weaving machines: they became an almost inexhaustible source of fuel for his stove.

Early in 1942, Avraham and Chaya received their 'wedding cards', our ghetto euphemism for resettlement notices. When they brought us the news, and heard that we were also to be moved, uncle could not contain his joy. 'You'll see, Gershon,' he declared with his ever-untamed exuberance, 'we'll go together. And no matter where to, no matter how small a room we'll get, I'll build another factory. We're brothers after all, and together we'll live through this difficult time in our lives.'

I can still picture my uncle's disappointment, the look on his grey face, the way he crawled into himself, when father told him a few days later that we had been excluded from this resettlement and were staying. The Bundist party, of which dad was among the oldest members in the ghetto, had devised a way to remove our names from the list. Families had to be resettled as complete units, and we had two infants, my two sisters' little girls; it was a cruel winter and they would not have been able to make the journey. The job of 'excluding' us was given to a young Bundist, Melech Wajsman. In the middle of the night, at the peril of his own life, he climbed through a window into the resettlement office, and by the light of a pocket torch removed the page on which our names appeared.

At the end of February it snowed, and the temperature dropped to perhaps 15 below zero. One morning at eight o'clock we went to say goodbye to our relatives. When we arrived we found uncle and aunt already sitting on a horse-drawn wagon with other people. On seeing my father, Avraham

jumped down. 'Gershon!' he shouted with unquenched enthusiasm. 'As soon as we get there, I'll write and let you know how
things are, and you can waste no time joining us.' Waving her
hand, Aunt Chaya cried 'Be well!' and the wagon drove off
towards the assembly point.

A month and a half went by without a word, without a hint
as to the whereabouts of our relatives or the other deportees.
Then, in April, a high-ranking officer sent by the commandant
at the Chelmno camp, in the town the Germans called Kulm-
hof, some 70 kilometres west of the city of the waterless river,
paid a surprise visit. He informed the Jewish ghetto admin-
istration – which quickly disseminated the happy news – that
our deportees were living contentedly there, and letters would
soon be forthcoming.

About six months later my mother, by now employed in
the official 'state laundry', found Uncle Avraham's jacket
among clothes that had arrived from various resettlements to
be cleaned. It was riddled with bullets, and in one of the
pockets was a scrap of paper with a single word scribbled in
blood: '*Chelmno*'.

❧ *Inner Freedom* ❧

My father, secular agnostic though he was, had his heart firmly
planted in tradition. Passover, he would say, is the annual celebration when we rekindle our collective memory of the Exodus,
mankind's first rebellion in the name of spiritual freedom.

April 1942 was a spring without a blade of grass, a spring
of skies without birds, while the very mice searched for food
across the futile land. In our iron stove, a drawer from our
wardrobe hummed its swan-song; yet come evening, a white
cloth and two lit candles made a bold appearance on a table

graced with emptiness. Father, in accordance with custom, had invited a friend to our Seder. A decent and noble man, Avraham Hirszfeld walked before God and had once belonged to that divine elite of whom it is written that not a word of theirs would the Lord let fall to the ground. But since January 1941, when his dying wife and two-year-old son had been sent to 'work' outside the ghetto, never to return, the quiet man who used to spend his life in prayer had turned into a disillusioned cynic.

Our guest seemed visibly indifferent to the occasion as we sat down to the Seder; perhaps he had come merely to escape his loneliness. But as father recited the familiar preamble — *'This is the bread of affliction which our ancestors ate in the land of Egypt. Let all who are hungry come and eat.'* — and lifted an imaginary *matzah* with his empty hand, Avraham unexpectedly erupted.

'Oh, please!' he cried out. 'Our Almighty well knows that no normal ghetto household possesses a crumb of food tonight, let alone bread. Why should we continue to delude ourselves?'

My wise father was quick to reply. 'Because here, illusions sustain us,' he said. 'What is true or false has only a theoretical significance — that is, no significance at all — and to be beholden merely to reality in a ghetto like ours is to commit…' He wouldn't say what. 'But let us continue, dear friend, with the beautiful myths embedded in our Passover story.' He resumed his reading, and we moved on to the *Ma Nishtana*, the great ritual question ('Why is this night different from all other nights?') with its four answers — the second of which concerned the eating of bitter herbs.

'Yes, yes,' our friend interrupted again, '*bitter* is the key word! I wonder how the future will understand our life, our sorrows, our mournful festivities — and more than anything, men like me who were willing to be lied to.'

'Please,' said father sternly. 'Let's continue.' And after the last answer had been given, he remarked: 'Leave the future to posterity, Reb Avraham. I can assure you that a hundred years from now Jews will sit around the *Pesach* table, eating a fine meal, and perhaps they will even place on the Seder plate one further ingredient, a potato-peel, in memory of our present calamity!'

We looked at Avraham, who seemed unconvinced. Father pressed on. '*We were slaves to Pharaoh in Egypt—*'

'So what has changed?' our guest retorted almost at once. Then, as if realizing at last that he was making a nuisance of himself, he raised his palm. 'Sorry, go on. I won't interrupt again.'

And so my father, the secular agnostic, continued his reading unabated, contributing occasional comments in relation to our present circumstances. And when he arrived at the end, he again inserted his own message. 'Next year, may the radiant light of our Passover guide humanity in its conquest of darkness.'

Mother rose from the table and a few moments later served us our Passover meal: a watery soup, garnished with a solitary potato-peel, which however kept cunningly evading my spoon.

Father smiled, looking at each of us in turn. 'The Jews will sing again,' he assured us, 'and they will read from our ancient *Haggadah* — though possibly with a slight addition to the text: '*And the Eternal brought us forth from Egypt, and indeed from the ghettos and the camps, not by means of an angel, not by means of a seraph, not by means of a messenger, but by Himself, the most holy, blessed be He in His glory.*'

Later, as he shook father's hand to leave, I heard the embittered Avraham remark: 'You seem visibly weary. Was it the reading or the sumptuous dinner?'

'Probably both,' father answered. 'Especially the latter.'

'So why do we do it?' Avraham just couldn't let go.

'To keep alive our inner sense of freedom,' said my father, gently closing the door.

≈ Linguistics ≈

Some sixteenth-century kabbalists believed that every word spoken by a righteous person created an angel. Evil words, on the other hand, begat devils. To confirm the truth of this postulation, they argued, one needed only to examine the language of the wicked.

Our German custodians in the ghetto — essentially an unsophisticated, unlearned lot — would not have been able to devise, on their own, a vocabulary that suited yet circumvented the finalities of purpose it had to denote. Luckily for them, there was no shortage of scholars in Berlin whose flow of words was prolific. These astute academicians zealously volunteered their services, and in no time at all they had begotten by daylight a night-tongue of deceit.

Resettlement became a virtual euphemism for murder. *Special handling* signified torture. To *come high* did not mean to be promoted, but to be hanged. To be *called up* was not to read from the Torah, but to be deprived of every last thing you had. Best of all, and definitely the most eloquent, was *Work will set you free* — free, that is, from life. Surely a stroke of sheer genius!

But it would be an extreme miscarriage of justice against Nazi ingenuity if one were not to include their seminal guiding principle — *Order*. Chaos had to be avoided at all costs, and the terminology must follow suit. This doctrine was perfectly exemplified by the ultimate directive: Distribute a towel and a piece of soap to each *figure* before the final entrance to the *showers*.

Once the doors were sealed, an official of the master race, notebook and pencil in hand, would ascend to the roof of this intricate invention, where the aspiring professor of linguistics could pin his blue eyes to the observation window, so as to record for posterity his academy's crowning achievement — the agony of dying children...

Guilt was not frequent among these peculiar devil-creators. They looked upon what they produced as a normal endeavour, an accepted industry within the system of their dream. The dream had spawned its own language, and the language nourished the dream.

❧ Suicide ❧

Like a wet smear, a rumour ran through the ghetto. A fearful and tangible murmur.

The Hunt.

The Germans, employing the Jewish police as their sniffer dogs, were about to strike at the very essence of our being. Nobody knew when; we knew only that all ghetto children under the age of ten and all adults over sixty-five would be taken, to be 'resettled'. We were accustomed to confronting death on a daily basis, but this latest perfidy caused the ghetto, that surreal asylum, to go berserk. Between 5 August and 5 September 1942, a plague of suicides — a spit in the face of creation — swept through our community.

Among these suicides was 27-year-old Kuna Leska, known after she married as Kuna Rotsztajn, who lived with her infant daughter Rifkele and her brother Gedaliah in a one-room apartment on the fifth floor of a nearby block. Like many others, Kuna had become acutely aware that her life was dangling from a cobweb's thread over a dark, bottomless abyss. She was alone:

in 1940 the Germans had conscripted her husband Michael to forced labour; a year later she was notified that he had 'died' in the course of his 'work'. Kuna was devastated; no doubt the blow nourished her psyche with murky solutions. And so, on that defeated sunny afternoon of 19 August, she jumped from her window into the liberating arms of death. Why she left her child behind is a question to which no one should seek an answer. Nothing will become clearer through explanation, and for the sake of a survivor's sanity it is dangerous even to ask.

Within a few minutes the paramedics (whose children, like those of the sniffer dogs, were exempt from the Hunt) arrived on the scene. Kuna's eyes were still open. The older of the two men gave her one glance, struck a match, sheltering the cigarette in the shell of his hands, and said: 'As good as gone. Take her away.'

The Hunt began on the morning of 5 September. As the huge high-sided truck rolled into the yard of 22 Łagiewnicka Street to collect the petrified little children, Gedaliah grabbed his niece, ran up to the roof, and roped her to the chimney in such a way that, for the duration of the search of their yard, she would appear as one with that structure. (He didn't have to warn the three-year-old fugitive not to cry.) Then Gedaliah turned his face to the sky: 'Almighty Lord,' he prayed, 'grant this child at least seven days of what my people granted You for all eternity — make her invisible!'

And He, may His name be forever blessed, did.

By the twelfth day of the month, the Hunt had come to a temporary pause. Gedaliah was just nineteen, his sister was dead, his parents in some nowhere, and he with a little girl to shelter, feed and protect. He decided to seek the help of his sister's sister-in-law, Dora Blatt. But as he entered her flat, holding Rifkele's thin hand in his, the woman and her husband Israel — a man who, once known for his composure, now resembled an asylum escapee — crumpled before him. 'Oh, Gedaliah, Gedaliah,' cried Dora. 'They took away *our* two children too, they've slaughtered us! We are dead!'

The young man understood the situation and left.

A few hours later, as the night was closing in, Dora unexpectedly appeared on Gedaliah's doorstep. She was dishevelled and her face bled from self-inflicted scratches. 'How will I sleep, Gedaliah? How *can* I sleep?' she wailed, taking the bewildered Rifkele by the hand and hugging her tightly to her breast. 'Maybe someone out there will have mercy on *my* children. After all, God is great…'

The little one, white as a ghost and trembling all over, as if suffering from an attack of malaria, could not contain herself any longer. 'Mummy!' she screamed. 'Mummy, *where are you, Mummy?*'

Her heart-wrenching plea would reverberate in her uncle's soul for the rest of his life.

So it was that, thanks to a distraught woman's nobility — and to Gedaliah's food-ration card, which he left with Dora — the good Lord endowed Rifkele with two more years of life and dread.

❦ *Give Me Your Children!* ❦

They reversed Leviticus. You shall steal. You shall deal falsely and deceitfully with one another. You shall commit robbery, defraud your neighbour. You shall withhold the wages of the labourer. You shall insult the deaf, place stumbling-blocks before the blind. You shall render unjust decisions, favour the rich, show no deference to the poor. You shall judge your kinsman unfairly, deal basely with your countryman, profit by the blood of your fellow. Keep these laws and do not fear God.

On 4 September 1942, in the third year of my barbed-wire existence, I heard our reigning puppeteer speak to the multitude. 'Mothers! Give me your children!' he pleaded.

> Yesterday afternoon, they gave me the order to send more than twenty thousand Jews out of the ghetto; if not, *We will do it for you!* So the question became, 'Should we take it upon ourselves, do it ourselves, or leave it to others to do?' Well, we — that is, I and my closest associates — had to think first not 'How many will perish?' but 'How many is it possible to save?' And we reached the conclusion that, however hard it would be for us, we must take the implementation of this decree into our own hands. I must perform this difficult and bloody operation — I must cut off limbs in order to save the body! I must take children because, if not, others will be taken as well, God forbid…

I wasn't a parent at the time, and perhaps I couldn't grasp fully the meaning of what I was witnessing. Yet more than six decades later, I still keep wondering what sort of a man can bring himself to utter such words.

Meanwhile, the 'resettling' commission — Rumkowski's appointees, whose children were not to be affected — sent out emissaries to weave stories and reassurances. All resettled youngsters would be placed in beautiful sunny kindergartens, while the sick and elderly would be under the care of famous German doctors. Do you really think, they argued vehemently, that people who walked with Mozart, Goethe and Beethoven could be capable of murdering babies?

My thirty-year-old friend Izzy Dajczman, with whom I worked at the factory at 13 Żabia Street, spoke little; when he did say something, you could hardly see his lips move. At the outbreak of war he had escaped to Russia with his wife Miriam and their little son Arele. He soon came back to occupied Poland, so as not to be late for his rendezvous with fate. 'To learn from one's mistakes is almost superhuman,' Izzy would whisper. At this time he and his family lived in a long, dark, one-window apartment which I often frequented. Miriam was a gentle soul and always greeted me with a smile.

The night of 5 to 6 September was a gruesome one for ghetto parents. At daybreak the Germans were to begin taking their children away, and there was nothing they could do. 'Let's hide,' Miriam pleaded. 'Let's hide no matter what.' But Izzy shook his head. 'If they catch us, we're *all* dead,' he said. 'So what? I'd rather be dead than give up my child!' 'What about the kindergartens? — maybe it's true...'

Mid-morning on 6 September. A Jewish policeman opens their door, enters, and lifts up Arele. The little fellow, white with fear, cannot understand why his mother is howling, why his father is shedding tears while reassuring her, 'Everything will turn out for the best, you'll see.' Arele is dressed in the new navy-blue woollen coat that his father made for his fifth birthday. On a wire around his thin neck hangs a piece of white linen with the boy's name and address: ARELE DAJCZMAN, KALLENBACH 6. 'Don't forget, Arele,' says Izzy as he walks him to the door, 'to tell your new teachers that you know both the Hebrew and the Latin alphabet, and that you already know numbers.'

Outside, a uniformed German grabs Arele by the collar and heaves him like a bundle of rags into a large waiting truck. Its open platform is walled in by several rows of timber planks, to crush any hope of escape for dangerous offenders like Arele Dajczman.

A few days later, on our way home from work, Izzy begs me to drop in for a minute, if only for Miriam's sake. 'She's down, so frightfully down,' he tells me. We climb the stairs and open the door to their room. A faint beam of light plays on Miriam, who is lying in bed with her face to the wall. As we draw nearer, we notice the pool of blood at her throat.

I spend a sleepless night in Izzy's flat. At the first spark of daylight I boil the kettle and we sit at the table, mourning in silence. At last I encourage him to eat a slice of bread. He obeys, and a few minutes later we go off to work together.

✒ The Pyramid ✒

In common with all hierarchies, our ghetto's social and functional organization — and its pecking order — was constituted in the shape of a pyramid. As the old saying goes, the deeper the foundations, the securer the structure.

The bedrock of the ghetto pyramid in the city of the waterless river consisted of tailors, cobblers, carpenters, weavers, hatters, plumbers, toolmakers, housepainters, barbers, and many others with less specialized hands. What was remarkable about the members of all these occupations is that, although they hated their masters, they loved to work — to mend, to make, repair, restore. Life was hard for the bedrock people, the load they carried on their meagre shoulders was heavy; yet many were the times when one would hear from the mouths of these starving toilers a tune hummed, a melody recalled, bringing back bygone days of humble happiness and family joy.

Szymon Berger was my foreman in the clothing factory, a smallish, upright, pedantic man, a tailor of some renown and an important stone in the pyramid's foundations. He taught me that happiness was an elusive commodity, difficult to trap. He had a twelve-year-old boy who was sick, and I observed in the factory how Szymon would never touch his soup; while the other workers ate heartily, he closed his eyes so as not to be tempted, and after work he would carry his meal, like a holy talisman of life, home to his sick son. Thinking back now, it reminds me of a disturbing story I once read, about a tigress that kept her cubs alive by feeding them with bits of meat ripped from her own body.

The next layer of the pyramid comprised an insipid host of inspectors, accountants, record-keepers, pen-pushers, notaries, and assorted squealers; inventors of 'evidence' who spent their days in whispers, beneath a barrage of lies.

Not far away, in fact on the layer just above them, were the cooks, the managers of public kitchens, the ladies with the lucky ladles, and the drab obtuse Jewish ghetto police. Next came the special units of the ghetto police, the dreaded Sonderkommando, responsible to the Germans and recruited mainly from among high-school students; perhaps because they were unable to shake off their feelings of inferiority, they terrorized those lower levels of the pyramid on which their very existence depended.

On the level before the pyramid's apex dwelt Rumkowski's trusted elite, who between them dreamt up an illusory inertia whereby the ghetto would remain just as it was, a nonexistent reality in which they refused to define themselves as victims.

At the top of the pyramid, then, was Mordechai Chaim Rumkowski, our king — whose eyes were like crows locked behind two thick-rimmed glass cages, and whose face appeared (at least to me) like a closed fist. He walked about the ghetto as if he owned it, but wore his sixty-odd years with a certain dignity. Although he had his trusted insiders to assist him, the ultimate decisions, the decisions of life and death — who would be resettled and who would stay behind — rested primarily on his shoulders. But where is the man who can state with conviction whether Rumkowski's decisions were a product of bravery or of cowardice? His lot was lonely, to be sure, and very far from easy. Did he have a choice? Perhaps he did, and perhaps he didn't. Our lives, after all, are determined by unknown chemistries, and governed by mysterious trajectories.

And in the end, who knows how many times, during sleepless nights, this man who projected such strength and confidence shrank back in horror at the echo of his own fateful words: 'Mothers, give me your children!'?

❧ *Mercy* ❧

There was a kind of unreality about my parents' friend, the tailor Fishl Binko. He seemed to be driven by a gregarious solitude, the simultaneous need to be in a crowd and to be alone. Fishl was also a great teller of fables — what a pity he never wrote any of them down. I can still remember a few.

A mountain-climber seeking shelter from the winds enters a little hut. The hut is filled with books, and its sole inhabitant, a philosopher sated with the years, welcomes him. 'Who are you, stranger?' he asks the climber. 'A wanderer, sir,' the other replies. 'Have you read any books, my young wanderer, have you any schooling?' 'No, sir.' 'Then please,' begs the old philosopher, 'tarry a little. I am in dire need of an honest teacher.'

Fishl was large and imposing of stature, with an olive complexion, and beneath his pitch-black bushy brows, his brown fathomless eyes and his sagging lips, he wore an expression of disenchantment. He had once been a great believer in justice and human decency, but the war, the ghetto, Europe's betrayal of his people, and awareness of our lives' permanent ephemerality — of which he didn't dare to speak, even to his closest, for fear of the very words — had transformed him into a fierce sceptic.

His wife Frumet, whom he had married in 1928, was a willowy woman from a traditional home, and four years his junior. She had an elongated face and rosy but slightly fallen cheeks. Her shiny dark-blond hair parted in the middle made her resemble, I thought, the image of a suffering Madonna, and not without reason. Like the biblical Hannah, Frumet had been plagued with barrenness; like Hannah, she had implored God in her wretchedness to open her womb. It took eight long and tearful years before the Almighty in His mercy finally answered her prayers.

Mirka was a beautiful, chubby child; thanks to her parents, even that starving ghetto of ours could not deprive her cheeks of their sweet dimples. As for Frumet, she was content with a few spoons of watery soup; her bread, to its last crumb, was put aside to nourish her growing Mirka, who by the autumn of 1942 was six years old.

When it was proclaimed early in September that all children under the age of ten were to be 'resettled', the whole family went into hiding. On the morning of the 7th, the Jewish police raided the Binkos' apartment. Satisfied with its deadly emptiness, they were about to leave when Mirka, who had been hidden under several layers of blankets, gave a little cough. Within seconds she was dragged from under the bedding. Fishl jumped to her rescue from his hiding-place but was swiftly knocked out. Then Frumet emerged, pounding away with both fists at the policemen's faces, screaming, 'My baby! My baby!'

Shortly afterwards the distraught, demented mother stood like a black hole in time before the ghetto fence. She had no more tears to cry, no voice left to scream with. Just beyond, on the outside, a little girl with a knapsack, holding on to her mother's hand, was walking to school; a boy was riding a bicycle; lovers were strolling, smiling, laughing... Of course, all this was an illusion. The only reality was the barbed-wire fence, and the guard. 'Take pity, merciful soldier, please,' she implored. 'Pull your trigger. Shoot me. Here, right here — right in my miserable heart!'

The guard duly obliged.

At night Fishl, like a sack emptied of its contents, sat on a low stool in the darkness, with ash on his head. Over and over, he was reciting a passage from the Bible:

Perish the day on which I was born,
And the night it was announced
'A male has been conceived!'
May that day be darkness;
May God above pay no heed to it;
May no light shine upon it;
May darkness and deep gloom reclaim it;
May a pall lie over it;
May what blackens the day terrify it.
May obscurity carry off that night;
May it not be counted among the days of the year…

So Fishl cursed the day of his birth, his life, his very being. But ghetto legend has it — and most of our legends are so rooted in reality that sometimes it's hard to tell which is which — that one night an angel paid him a visit. 'Fishl,' he said. 'God admits that he sinned against you. He is about to give you a new wife, and *three* Mirkas. Remember Job?'

'No, no!' the stricken man answered. 'Go back to God and tell Him that Fishl Binko is overburdened with His mercies.'

'What do you intend to do?' asked the angel, growing uneasy.

'Hang myself.'

'That would be to defy the Master?'

'So be it.'

'But Fishl, all those who committed suicide in the ghetto are walking around in Hell.'

'That may be true. But their faces are shining.'

❧ *History Lesson* ❧

At the height of their victories the Germans stood at the gates of Moscow, while we Jews, a multitude of emaciated shadows, were incarcerated in a twilight crevice awaiting the end of our days. Father, albeit the eternal pessimist, said: 'Yes, they may enter Moscow, even push beyond, but they will lose the war.'

'What makes you say that?' asked my mother, surprised. 'Look at them, Gershon! Look at their mobility, their armour, their tanks and guns. Each of them is like a god of war. Who is there to match their power? In no time, they have become masters of Europe.'

'You're right,' father replied, his grey eyes like two eagles in flight on his knotted parchment face. 'But there is an anecdote from history that throws a strong light on the present situation. During his pursuit of the cunning Kutuzov, Napoleon spotted through his spyglass a Russian ulan softening his stale bread in his stallion's urine. He lowered his glass, turned to one of his generals, and said, "We've lost the war!" You see, these Russians can trade misery for machines, space for speed, and what the invaders have forgotten is that Berlin's pleasant tradition of afternoon *Kaffee und Kuchen* is not upheld that far to the east — especially when the thermometer tells them, "Gentlemen, put your noses in your pockets, it's 50 degrees below zero."

We smiled but father was just warming up. 'And yet,' he continued, 'the Führer's press chief, Otto Dietrich, summoned the foreign press in October last year to announce officially that, for all practical purposes, the war was won! On account of such a glorious victory, Reichsidiot Adolf Schicklgruber dismissed nineteen of his most able generals and appointed himself commander-in-chief of the army. You see, Masha, this evil fool obviously believes that military strategy and street-brawling, at which he was once an expert, are one and the same thing.

'No, the Germans will definitely lose the war,' my ever-doubting father repeated unequivocally, 'and those who live to witness humanity's triumph will also witness the way these once-pompous and arrogant Teutons will run like frightened rats to the seven corners of the world.'

'What then?' I spoke up at last. 'After everything that has happened, will mankind quietly return to the same old way of thinking — complete with all their ideologies, dogmas, beliefs?'

'Yes. And do you know why? Because Sancho Panza cannot live without Don Quixote. Because one illusive beacon in a hopeless night is worth a thousand daylight suns.'

The late afternoon was bending toward dusk, our room darkened. Mother lit the kerosene lamp; she knew how father loved its smoky flame. It reminded him of his childhood home, his mother Perl Gittel, his strict religious father, the melamed Yeruchim, who would sit day and night studying the scriptures. For a good while, dad stood before the flame like one in prayer, and as his lean shadow began to sway on our green wall, I heard him take up a soft chant.

There is a time for everything,
*   and a season for every purpose under heaven:*
A time to be born and a time to die,
A time to plant and a time to uproot,
A time to kill and a time to heal,
A time to destroy and a time to build,

A time to weep and a time to laugh,
A time to mourn and a time to dance,
A time to cast stones and a time to gather them,
A time to embrace and a time to refrain,
A time to search and a time to give up,
A time to keep and a time to discard,
A time to tear and a time to mend,
A time to be silent and a time to speak,
A time to love and a time to hate,
A time for war and a time for peace.

And as an afterthought, he added: 'In peace we prepare for war, and in war for another war. Madness has no seasons.'

☞ *Metamorphosis* ☜

Gerhard Reimer was born in the deep north-east, beyond the Gulf of Riga, where moons like lost yellow ships anxiously searched the interminable oceanic expanse of black skies for a secure port of call.

When he was eight his father, Herman Reimer, sent him away to a boarding school in Tallinn, where he was taught many useful things: mastery of the German tongue, discipline, songs, and nightly drillings. 'Don't saunter!' his marching instructor shouted. 'Saunterers think. Soldiers shouldn't!' Although little Gerhard *was* always thinking — for he was intelligent and perceptive — he nevertheless had no problem obeying his new teachers. Obedience had been an integral part of his strict upbringing.

Gerhard grew into an exceptionally handsome young man. At twenty-one he was an upright Christian, and a decorated leader of the Hitler Youth. He wore shiny black boots, a brown shirt, and a red armband adorned with a black cross bent into hooks (at times he wondered how Jesus would have looked on a cross like that). He still hadn't forgotten those fearful nights when he heard Mama in the adjoining room grappling with Papa in their bed; and how one frosty winter's night he, little Gerhard, had crawled out of his own warm bed and knelt before the crucifix on the wall, praying that his father might show his mother some mercy.

One morning in December 1942, when the earth was painted with a coat of snowflakes, there was a knock on the door of Gerhard's comfortable apartment, which had belonged to a Jewish doctor who had been sent away. Clicking his heels and calling *Heil Hitler!*, he jumped to attention before the two uniformed officers, who politely but curtly asked him to hop into the car waiting outside.

They journeyed for hours without exchanging a word. Gerhard didn't mind, he was used to war games and secret missions. Gazing out languidly at the snowy Christmas landscape hurtling past, he dozed off, and all at once he could hear his parents in their bed again, and mother's whimpers and pleas, and he saw his homely cloud-streaked moon, but this time it was poking out at him an enormous slimy red tongue…

They arrived mid-morning and were greeted subserviently by an elderly gentleman. On his nose rested a pair of brown horn-rimmed spectacles; he wore a grey hat, a black-and-white herringbone coat — and a yellow star on his chest! 'What's this?' cried Gerhard, reaching for his scout knife. 'Are there still Jews left in our new Reich?'

'Hold it, hold it!' commanded his humourless escort. He relieved Gerhard of his weapon. 'From now on,' he said, 'you will do as this man tells you.'

'But why?' Gerhard shouted in desperation. 'Please, it's all a big mistake — what have I to do with these people?'

'You'll have to ask your grandfather's father,' responded one of the escorts. They jumped into the car and drove off in a cloud of dust.

Two Jewish policemen respectfully chaperoned Gerhard to his new quarters, where he threw himself on the cold bunk and cursed, screamed, wept, and perhaps thought of escaping. But the habit of obedience would not permit him even now to rebel against authority, and after a month or two of self-isolation Gerhard bowed his head before the Eldest, the man with the yellow star who had welcomed him, and embarked on his career as a weaver in Kaszub's textile factory.

At first he was rather confused. He had never seen Jews like this — gaunt, haggard, yet upright and proud Jews, some of them even good-looking. Even their noses looked normal! Oh, heavens, they must all be like me, he thought, neither Gentile nor Jew. And there behind one of the huge machines he spotted my former school friend — petite, dark-eyed, with waves of shoulder-length auburn hair — the beautiful Debora, whose white skin would have been the envy of many a fine Aryan lady. Was she Jewish too? He soon found himself wondering what she thought of *him*. And so, after days of curiously searching each other's faces, there began to grow a longing for words, and then for the touch of hands.

Gerhard took a strong liking to Debora's wise father, David Wajnberg, who spoke about his Jewish agnosticism with a great deal of pride; who, with reference to many historical examples, pointed out that nations which had oppressed Jews had always written out their own curse; who, despite all the setbacks, believed that the only way for humanity to survive was through socialism. Lying on his bunk at night, Gerhard pondered his life, his flame for Debora, his attachment to her father, the meaning of destiny, and his mysterious bond to these ghetto people of whom he had known so little...

In September 1945, on a sunny morning in Rome, I was strolling near the Piazza d'Espagna when I came upon my old friend Debora. Her face, against the blue Roman sky, looked paler than it really was, and her black eyes much blacker. We practically fell on each other, and stood for a good while locked in a tender embrace. With an almost mischievous smile, she invited me to visit her room.

After an arduous climb up a precipitous winding staircase, we stood in an unlit corridor. I could sense Debora's tension, and thought I detected the old fire in her eyes as she reached for the key that was hanging on a chain around her neck. Quickly she unlocked the squeaky door, and there — oh, my God, there on an army bunk, white as a ghost, lay Gerhard Reimer! He was somewhat astonished to see me, but his greeting was warm and friendly. We drank hot coffee without exchanging a word. There are times when silence is the most natural condition. When I rose to say goodbye I kissed Debora more fully on the lips than I should have, and noticed the jealous glint in Gerhard's eyes.

'Please forgive him for not getting up from the bunk,' she whispered. 'He is in agony. You see, it's just the third day after his circumcision.'

∾ *Riddles* ∾

My former schoolmate Yossele, who had assisted our sport teacher Laibl Grundman in burying within the schoolyard a list containing the names of all our school's students, a kind of time-capsule, was a fellow of simple language and complex ideas. Yossele espoused the theory that there were no grey areas in life, everything was either black or white. Outside of that equation, he declared with his characteristic extremity, dwelt only the absurd.

Yossele maintained that the central pillar of our social structure was hypocrisy. Without it our system would collapse, he said, like a house of cards on a windy day. Adam and Eve, he further argued, had sewn leaves together to make not loin-cloths but masks. Those masks, he proclaimed triumphantly, had transformed the earth into a living paradise!

Yossele was fond and proud of his Yiddish school, which he completed just before the outbreak of the war. His secondary education would be the ghetto, his university Auschwitz, and he would gain his postgraduate credentials from prestigious Bergen-Belsen, with high distinctions in remembering.

I had lost contact with Yossele in 1939, not long before we were all consumed by that cataclysm of blood and fire. It was in New York that I met him again, many years later, in a room full of strangers. He was happy only when he spoke about his miseries: life in camp, the beatings, betrayals, how he was sold for a kilo of sugar, his interrogation by the Gestapo, his escape, the night he spent in a kennel with a dog — probably an angel, he explained.

But when he spoke of how, one summer's night, he had been caught by some villagers and hung by his legs from a cherry tree, he just couldn't stop laughing. People thought he was crazy. What they didn't realize was that Yossele was reliving his youth.

∾ *The Absence* ∾

The architects of our inverted state had a tremendous aptitude for social geography: most of the ghettos they established were sheltered from military activities, safe and secure amid a wider populace not averse to lending a hand in the achievement of their masters' final solution.

My daring street friend Leon Ronski walked about the world with a snub nose, a straw-white mane, and eyes like an unblemished summer sky. One morning he noticed his father — the pious and respected Szachna Ronski, a giant of a man — sitting in a corner and sobbing like a child. 'He hasn't eaten for three days,' Leon's mother told him. 'He just can't bear it any more. I begged him to take *my* slice of bread, but he'd rather die than do that.'

As soon as dusk fell Leon rushed to the edge of the ghetto, sneaked out through the barbed wire and boarded the last tram to the outskirts of a nearby village, where the granaries were bursting at the seams and virtually every home baked its own bread. He waited until the people were sleeping soundly, took off his shoes, and was about to put his plan into motion when the faithful village dogs picked up the scent of an intruder. Within minutes the whole place was on its feet. Men, women and children ran out into the night, all in their underwear, armed with torches and pitchforks, screaming '*Żyd, żyd, żyd!*' Leon was caught soon enough, sitting in the branches of a tree he had managed to climb into. Naturally, the honour of dealing with the trespasser was given (principally) to the one who had spotted him first. Fair is fair.

Two days later, battered and bloodied all over, Leon was marched back at gunpoint to the edge of the ghetto. The guards released him and ordered him to run. Then, as he was about to scale the fence, one of them sent a bullet through his head. The Jewish police were told to notify his parents that he had been shot trying to escape from custody.

Just before the news was brought to him, Reb Szachna happened to be studying the Bible, and had reached the twenty-eighth chapter of Genesis. He closed his eyes, reciting verses 20 and 21 from memory:

And Jacob made a vow, saying: 'If God remains with me, and protects me on this journey that I am making, and gives me bread to eat and clothing to wear, so that I return safe to my father's house, then the Lord shall be my God.'

Something caused Szachna to open his eyes, and his gaze fell on the open *Tanach*. He uttered a cry. The two verses that he knew so well were missing, and in their place there gaped an absence as blank as despair.

✺ *Rabbi Chaskele* ✺

I learnt about Rabbi Chaskele and his fate from the rabbi's nephew, Kalman, a Talmudist in his own right. While we were queuing for bread early one winter's morning, the young man, rubbing his frozen hands together and stamping his cold feet, sang an infectious old Yiddish folksong under his breath:

Yidl with his fiddle,
Arieh with his bass,
Life is but a little song,
Why then make a fuss?

I chuckled; we exchanged some words, and soon found ourselves chatting like old friends. Before long Kalman was telling me his story — which I quickly realized was merely a brief shortcut to that of his uncle. 'I came here from a nearby shtetl,' he said, 'where, in a cluster of white houses huddling like forlorn sheep on a piece of land that was once green pasture, lived a few thousand Jews. Their elder, their doyen, was my frail widowed uncle Chaskel the kabbalist, known as "Chaskele" because he was so incredibly tiny. In our time of harsh and bitter realities, Chaskel could withdraw into his own dream world. He had many sayings. "Kalman," he would tell me, "creation does not exist for its own sake, but for the sake of the shining force of the Creator." You see, one has to be good to give new meaning to old truths, and my uncle, whom I loved like a father, really was good.'

My new friend paused, drew a deep breath. 'A day before Purim, two men in black uniforms came to see my uncle. They demanded ten Jews for a *Spiel*, a 'show', to be staged in the marketplace at dawn the next day. Uncle told them that he would be there; the other nine they would have to find for themselves. By way of deposit they gave him a beating, and left. I knew what to expect. All night long I begged him to run for his life but he wouldn't hear of it. Only frauds, phony leaders, ran away from their communities in times of peril, he said. I argued that there was no logic in his staying. Maybe, he agreed, but too much logic was sometimes tantamount to absurdity! Desperate, infuriated, I cried: "For God's sake, uncle, what are you trying to achieve?" My uncle nodded. "Yes, Kalman," he answered, "precisely for God's sake have I endeavoured, all my life, to instruct men in righteous deeds, not in those that are merely speculative or convenient." I knew he was right, but how could I let it go at that? "What you say is true," I told him, "but it has little to do with the grim reality staring you in the face today." For a good while my uncle, the sharp kabbalist, said nothing. I thought he was about to succumb. Instead, this frail man who fasted every Monday and Thursday pushed his face close to mine and whispered into my ear: "Kalman, my son, the song of light in its dialogue with darkness does not need to authenticate itself in accordance with existing realities."

'An eerie dimness hovered over the marketplace on that godforsaken dawn. The whole community, having been ordered to assemble around the gallows, watched anxiously as Rabbi

Chaskele emerged from his house. Behind him walked nine elderly Jews, who had spent the night in prayer. They walked firm and upright, their heads held high. "Look, it's a miracle, a miracle," someone murmured. "Our Rabbi Chaskele is growing taller every moment! Look, can you see? Soon he'll reach the heavens!"

'As a soldier placed the noose around my uncle's neck, Chaskele whispered, almost plaintively: "Perhaps you will permit me one last wish. I would like to touch the officer in charge." The soldier laughed. "Why would you want to do that?" he sneered. "I don't mean any harm, sir," Chaskele replied. "I just want to ascertain if this man, too, has been created in God's image."'

❧ *Elegy for a Little House* ❧

It stood alone, at 12 Limanowskiego Street, a modest two-storey timber dwelling with four bashful windows, on its pitch-black roof a happy chimney wearing a smoky wig. It looked small beside the neighbouring four-storey block where I lived. Yet it housed four families, each behind a friendly open door. Upstairs was a glazier with his diminutive wife and five children; next to them, a widowed cobbler with a daughter and a son, the boy unable to speak because he was born with a split on his upper lip. The ground floor was occupied by Noah the baker, whose wife had borne him three daughters and three sons, all master bakers; and across the unlit passage lived Itche-Meier the stationer, who spent every free moment studying the Bible with his black cat Fraidl sitting in his lap, and had a son called David, a violinist.

I loved these people — the glazier with his family; the widowed cobbler visited at dusk by a string of nocturnal ladies;

fat Noah, a small mountain of flesh wobbling about on two tiny sticks, his wife who despised daylight, the three boys I played poker with, the three plump daughters who spent most of their time in my fantasies; and the stationer Itche-Meier, from whom I kept stealing ping-pong balls. Above all I adored David, and passed many pleasant after-school hours on his back step, where my ears became attuned to the autumnal sadness of his strings.

I remember the day a rowdy mob attacked the quiet defenceless panes of the little house with a hail of stones, and then with bricks. It stood its ground, and all through the bombardment, to my astonishment, David resolutely continued playing his violin.

So summer turned to autumn, and autumn was overtaken by winter — a winter which afflicted men's tongues with a new language of perfidy and violence. Amid the darkness, even the best of us found it hard to find a consoling word, yet there were those who still argued that the war was about to end. It seemed to me that 'my' little house, which I cherished, understood better. It is not good to talk oneself into impossible fictions, so the house, like a frightened snail, receded into itself.

There was no tramstop in front of the little house, yet the afternoon came when a green Number 8 tram nevertheless halted there. Three young Germans, their guns trained, swiftly alighted. After roughing up the inhabitants of the house, they took them all away. It was to be a journey of no return.

That night I was awoken by footsteps, the squeaking and banging of doors opening and closing, and the suppressed voices of a throng of haggard men who had left their sick wives and children around unheated stoves in freezing homes. Stealthily they walked the snow-white paths, and with crowbars and axes they assailed the little house for what timber they could plunder, until nothing remained.

I would often visit this scene of devastation in my dreams, hoping for a sign of life; but to no avail. One night in spring I unexpectedly came upon a tiny green leaf of grief, wet with dew. 'It's true,' it said, 'there's nothing left of what once was. But listen — each night they all come back, their souls in white shrouds. I cannot see their faces, but I can hear their voices and their ghostlike steps, as soft as Fraidl's paws on the prowl. They never tarry; perhaps they still fear for their life even in death, who can tell? Last time they came I begged David to play, to play once again the story of his little house. He apologized. Ashmodai had tossed his violin into the fire. But he said the melody had escaped the flames. Next time, he promised, he would teach me the song.'

≈ *Holy Lies* ≈

My friend Kuba Litmanowicz, a toolmaker by trade, was a man of enormous physical strength, great loyalty, few words, and deep, shining thoughts. He was also a lover of the sun. His build and his olive skin always reminded me of the Yiddish verses of Moyshe Kulbak:

> *Young men of bronze*
> *impelled by a will*
> *to appease the anger*
> *of years that have flown —*
>
> *Come, let us go,*
> *let us leave the weaklings behind…*

But now Kuba was dying. Ghetto hunger had brought on tuberculosis. He knew it was the end, yet here he was, pleading:

'Tell me a lie. Please tell me they are losing the war, it will make it so much easier to die.'

'There's no need to lie,' I reassured him. A few of us were standing around his bed. 'They *are* losing the war, and you'll live to see it.'

'Thanks, friend,' he smiled. 'I still have the talent to surrender to fantasies, to be utterly deceived by dreams. You know I was always a free-thinker, but now, with this body becoming a battleground of life and death, I've come to understand that there is nothing stronger within us, nothing mightier, than that mysterious force of which we know nothing…'

For a good minute he kept his eyes closed. I felt a stab in my heart, fearing that they had closed for the last time. But suddenly they opened again, alive, larger and wider than ever, gleaming blue-gold, like the bright flames of two dwindling candles.

'I read once,' he said, in a voice that was almost unearthly, 'a poem written by a Hungarian poet whose name I've forgotten. A mother is speaking to her son, who has been condemned to death. "I have been granted an audience with our young king," she tells him. "I'll bow my grey head before him, kiss his feet, and beg for your life, my only one. When you climb the steps up to the gallows, turn your eyes towards our balcony. I'll be standing there, and if you see a black scarf around my neck, you will know, my son, that your mother failed you; but if the scarf is white, as I am sure it will be, you'll know, my son, that mercy has been granted."

'And so, at dawn the next morning, the young man walks towards the gallows, the bleak sea of his life raging about him, rising and falling between *to be* and *not to be*. As he climbs the final step, where the treacherous noose hangs ready to cradle his head, he cautiously turns to the balcony where his mother stands, waving her hand. And there, about her neck — Oh God, the scarf of life!

'He pauses for a moment, then radiantly steps up to the rope, where shortly he will swing with a smile on his youthful lips.'

➤ My Aunt's Candlesticks ➤

My mother's sister, Esther Hinda, was renowned for her piety, but she had a bitter life. Her husband, my uncle Shlomo, who kept a shoe shop at Nowomiejska 28, was a chain-smoker and an incorrigible scoffer at religion. According to the beadle at our local synagogue, Shlomo paid the price: in 1935 he contracted cancer and the following year he was off to face his Maker. His departure was excruciating, but my uncle was also stubborn and stoical, and refused to complain. His doctor, Herszkowicz, a man with murderous grey eyes, and hands that looked as though they were forever soaked in soapy water, begged him: 'Please, Shlomo; moan, cry, scream — it'll be easier.' But the patient wouldn't hear of it. 'No, doctor. Dying is not an art, but to die like a man *is*.'

After my uncle's death Hinda and her five daughters inherited the shoe shop, but none of them had any idea about the business so things went from bad to worse. As luck would have it, soon after the Germans seized our city of the waterless river they assigned the shop to a prominent and meticulous compatriot, who quickly relieved the family of its services, then secretly placed my aunt's name on a list of the city's well-to-do.

On Kościelna Street, amid leafy trees behind St Mary's Church, there stood a two-storey redbrick house occupied by the criminal police, known as the 'Kripo'. Jews who had the misfortune to be interrogated in that bastion of justice seldom came out in one piece. On a wintry Monday, just after reciting her morning prayers, Esther Hinda received an invitation to the aforesaid house to declare her wealth.

'Apart from my engagement ring,' the frightened woman stuttered, 'my earrings, and five silver coins with the image of Józef Piłsudski, I have nothing to declare.' Two hefty slaps on the face and a blow to her belly from Sutter, the man in charge, made Hinda spit out her dentures, which contained a number of teeth capped with gold. 'Aha!' said the master interrogator, who spoke Yiddish as capably as any Jew. 'If you open your mouth voluntarily, you'll get off lightly. Aren't you aware that we know everything about you? Of course I'll accept your jewellery without qualms, *and* your Piłsudski coins, but to hold back from us your famous candlesticks would be nothing short of sheer *chutzpah*.' Sutter smiled meaningfully. 'Now strip!' he shouted, knocking off her wig.

Standing naked in the freezing windowless room, her small hands covering her private parts, Hinda looked like a frightened, emaciated boy. One nod from Sutter and his gang of three bullies began rhythmically to punch her tiny body. But she would sooner have parted with her life than with the Sabbath candlesticks which her forefathers had saved from the fires of Lisbon, and her foremothers had carried, like babes enveloped in prayer-shawls, through Venice, Paris and Amsterdam, until they brought them to this land of her birth.

Every Friday in the ghetto, after her children had escaped to Russia at the outbreak of war, Hinda would cautiously descend through the trapdoor under her bed into a dark musty basement. She would spread a white cloth over an empty wooden crate, pull the candlesticks from their hiding-place and light two candles, covering her eyes with her hands as tears rolled down her sunken cheeks. She would chant: '*Blessed art thou, Lord out God, King of the universe, who hast sanctified us with Thy commandments, and commanded us to kindle the Sabbath lights.*'

How she must have longed for the peace and solitude of that basement as, over three long days, Hinda was kicked, bludgeoned and whipped by Sutter and his cronies; but she would not give in. On the fourth day, lying naked on the floor, bleeding from her ears, nose and mouth, as Sutter yet again brought his booted foot against her thin neck, she heard the voice of her father, Aba Bresler: *Esther Hinda, daughter mine, for God's sake remember* Pikuach nefesh — *life above everything.*

That was when my aunt finally relented.

Sutter had the candlesticks promptly retrieved and brought to him. He studied the inscription engraved under the base of each of the ancient pieces: '*Porto Israel, Lisboa 1457,*' he read out. 'I knew your family wouldn't collect any junk.' Excitedly he called out to his henchmen to join the ceremony. What happened then we know only from an account given by a Jewish charlady who witnessed the scene through a door left slightly ajar.

Hinda, naked and in pain, was forced to put a burning match to two candles that had been placed in the candlesticks. According to the distraught witness, the moment she did this, two enormous black tongues of flame burst from the sacred objects. My aunt's face turned ash-pale, and she started to chant not the blessing for light but the mourner's prayer: '*Magnified and sanctified be His great name...*' She stopped abruptly, hit the floor, and never got up.

❧ *Surreal* ❧

Today, Herszke Goldstern, a 41-year-old worker, hanged himself in his apartment at 16 Wróbla Street. Adolf Epstein, aged 42, resettled here from Sudetenland, also hanged himself in his apartment at 35 Zawiszy Street. The mother, 43, of Fajga

Paciorek, a school friend of mine, jumped from a third-storey window at 63 Lutomierska Street. And Julius Borhard, in his mid-seventies, slashed his veins and leapt from the window of the old people's home.

A major arrest was made. A plainclothes policeman discovered a secret workshop producing pancakes from rotten vegetables and potatoes retrieved from garbage. The two families involved, residing at 13 Lwowska Street, were preparing this delicacy most probably for profit; both families were arrested by order of the public prosecutor. In the course of the investigation the prisoners denied that they had engaged in the sale of the pancakes, but one of their children spilled the beans. 'We employed a salesman,' the little boy innocently revealed.

Last night, at the House of Culture, the concert conducted by David Bajgelman played to a capacity audience. Chairman Rumkowski, flanked by his faithful entourage, sat in the front row. The orchestra accompanied a singer in her rendition of some Yiddish songs, then presented several works from the classical repertoire. The climax was a rousing performance of a Beethoven piano concerto.

At the conclusion of the program a delighted chairman made a fine speech appropriate to the occasion. Afterwards, Rumkowski took aside one of his trusted assistants, Szaja Stanisław Jakobson, and asked him to summon the soloist.

'*Di host shain geshpielt*,' he told the young man in Yiddish. 'You played well. But why do you look so pale?'

'I lost my wife, sir, to typhus, just two weeks ago,' the pianist answered nervously. 'I lost her,' he repeated.

'I know how it feels,' said the chairman. 'I also lost my beautiful wife, in the prime of her life. She used to sing the Yiddish songs I heard here tonight.' Rumkowski had tears in his eyes. Briskly he turned to his assistant. 'Szaja,' he shouted, 'see that the *muzykant* gets a double portion of soup for the next two weeks. And make sure the doctor gives him a script for a weekly ration of potato-peels, but from the police kitchen — don't forget, Szaja, it must only be from the police kitchen.'

The night outside was windy and drizzly when the chairman left the concert hall. I happened to be standing nearby. In his dark coat, and with thick black-rimmed spectacles perched on his Roman nose, Rumkowski appeared to me like a lonely owl. Despite his sixty-odd years, he climbed quite nimbly into his *droshka*. He signalled to the coachman and the brown old nag took off. I don't know why, but the rhythmic clatter of its hoofs made me think of a wagon rumbling towards an ever-hungry guillotine.

∼ *Family Friends* ∼

The Rabanovs were old family friends. Josef had been my father's comrade-in-arms at the time of the 1905 revolution. They had stood shoulder to shoulder defending the barricade on Wschodnia Street, in the city of the waterless river, against the onslaught of the Tsar's cossacks. Josef was unusually tall, and therefore known among the conspirators as 'Long Jos', while father was 'Little Gershon'. Both were textile weavers by profession.

Despite his proletarian status, Josef was always immaculately dressed: black jacket, dark pinstriped trousers and, on weekends, aristocratic white gloves. A yellowish smudge on his thick silver-grey moustache betrayed his addiction to tobacco. His wife Berenice was a petite brunette, well-shaped, with long brown hair, deep-set eyes and a face like that of a white porcelain doll. Berenice always wore a black shirt-dress trimmed with white silk, and spoke with a throaty but pleasing voice accompanied by lively gesticulation — often she would shape her hands and long fingers into a ball, as if to round off her message or perhaps lend global meaning to her thoughts. She had once been a celebrated actress on the Yiddish stage, where she learnt the beautiful art of merging truth with imagination. The simplest utterance, when imbued with her diction and style, became a festive, a Godly event.

I never tired of hearing her memorable story about the opening night of a well-known drama. 'We premiered in a disused hall, and as the curtain rose, revealing a dilapidated little synagogue where two starved disciples pondered the coming of the Messiah, a stray black cat happened to cross the stage, stopped in the centre, scanned the astonished audience with resentful green eyes, then haughtily lifted its bushy tail and continued on. The morning papers were mad with excitement, praising this accidental occurrence as the dramatic effect of the twentieth century!'

The Rabanovs were childless and very much in love. Josef, not unlike his biblical predecessor, was full of dreams; some of them even came to fruition. My father, an incurable sceptic, grew to love his friend's fantasies in the ghetto — perhaps, in our hopelessness, they offered relief from the futilities of everyday life. Although the war radically changed the pattern of our existence, the Rabanovs kept visiting us twice a week, on Sundays and Wednesdays after work, as they had always done.

December 1942 was a gloomy month. The devastating news from the front choked what was left of our waning spirit. In the north, the Germans lay like a boa at the throat of our allies' great city of Leningrad. Moscow was about to do a Kutuzov. The harsh winter got into father's bones and froze his joints; the pain was excruciating and he took to his bed. On his visits Josef would sit hunched in a chair beside him.

'Gershon, listen,' he would announce excitedly, 'I had another dream, a glorious dream. I saw a mighty army, like some terrible primordial glacier, rise out of Moscow. It advanced with incredible speed, overrunning the panic-stricken Germans, squashing them like lice.' My father would shake his head: 'Oh Jos, Jos, will it ever come to pass?' 'It will, Gershon, it will, and we'll be there to see it!'

The long hard winter that year was accompanied by a cruel famine, a famine that produced a bountiful harvest of death. It catapulted the gravediggers into an enviable elite: people gave away their last crumb of bread just to have their loved ones buried. One Thursday in late January it snowed all day long, and that night there was a knock on our door. It was Berenice. She looked distraught, and I knew something horrible had happened. Taking mother aside, she began in a hushed voice, though the dancing shadows of her gesticulating hands on the dimly-lit wall spoke clearly enough of an insurmountable inner struggle. Soon she had abandoned her whispers. 'How could he, how could he do this?' she cried.

'You have to talk to him,' mother was saying. 'To steal bread in ghetto—'

'Oh please, please, don't use that word — my Josef is no thief!... I knew I shouldn't have come here, but I just had to share my anguish with someone...'

'You mustn't despair,' mother tried to console her. 'It's become an almost daily occurrence.'

'Yes — and after all, it was only me he took the bread from, and he says he was going to replace it as soon as he got his next ration...'

Well, Josef was unable to tame his hunger, and a darkness descended upon the Rabanovs' once loving relationship, a painful estrangement. Virtually overnight the upright heroic dreamer became a *klepsydra* — ghetto term for a walking death-notice — and the lively Berenice had become the tragic protagonist of a miscarried drama. The Rabanovs stopped visiting our home. My parents suffered, for they loved their lifelong friends and father missed Josef's sanguine effervescence.

Dad was the oldest Bundist in the ghetto, so when the party celebrated its forty-sixth jubilee he was asked to deliver a lecture. It took place in an attic somewhere on Łagiewnicka Street; his topic was *Yiddish and Socialism*. Towards the end of father's speech a smart-alec in the audience called out: 'Comrade Gershon, perhaps you might like to tell us, which are you first, a Yid or a socialist?' My father didn't skip a beat. 'As far as I know,' he replied, 'I was circumcised before I ever heard of Karl Marx.' The room broke into laughter. Afterwards, as an expression of gratitude for a well-delivered oration, the organizers bestowed on father a magnificent prize: a voucher from the Bund kitchen for two kilos of potato-peels. Next day I redeemed the voucher. Mother immediately set to work, and in no time had produced a cake fit for a royal feast. When she was about to serve, she asked me to run across to the Rabanovs and ask them to join us in this unexpected banquet.

The door to their flat was not locked, but the threshold was ice. Inside, the windows were covered with dark curtains, the walls coated with a glistening frost. There was not a stick of furniture in the place, except for the wrought-iron bed on which the Rabanovs were resting. I approached on tiptoe, so as not to wake them too abruptly.

They lay in an inseparable embrace, Josef with wide-open bewildered eyes and Berenice with her face buried in her husband's breast. Her graceful arms, thin and lily-white, were pleated around his neck like a noble wreath of forgiveness.

✎ *Red Rebecca* ✎

My niece Frumetl attended the same kindergarten as I did, but
sixteen years later. What is remarkable about that is the fact
that we both took our first steps in the outside world under the
guidance of the same teacher. Miss Fela, adored by us less for
her rare intellect than for the special sense of safety she radi-
ated, was of indeterminate age. In her eyes she carried the love
of an angel; on her small back she carried a prominent hump.

Until the middle of 1942 she still ran her kindergarten at
34 Zgierska Street, though after Rumkowski's 'Give me your
children' speech, she was left with just one little girl, Frumetl. As
things went from bad to worse, as Germans in collusion with
our local agents kept snooping about the clandestine kindergartens, my sister preferred to keep her child in a dark unused
room with a rusty old padlock on the door.

I nevertheless returned every fortnight, as I always had, to
visit my teacher of old. In Miss Fela's kindergarten room
stood an aquarium, where, once beloved of all the children,
Red Rebecca still hid among the weeds of her green world.
On my visits I would change the water and clean the aquarium. In former days it had been a great honour for any child
to be in charge of Red Rebecca's needs, since the goldfish was
regarded by all as a real person.

I enjoyed coming to see the teacher of my formative years.
Despite the difficulties and the shortages, there was always a
hot cup of tea, a slice of brown cake baked from burnt wheat-
chaff, and a good talk. On one such occasion, as she looked
out through a small window upon our narrow world, Miss
Fela observed: 'Those who believed that, thanks to education,
brutality would become a thing of the past, made a mistake
with a capital M. It seems to me that man's insanity is carried
along by its own peculiar inertia.'

It is January 1943, an unbearably frosty winter morning. The angel of death, white and freezing, is impatiently jumping up and down on people's doorsteps. I run up the kindergarten stairs. The door stands surprisingly open. I dash in. Miss Fela is sitting on a low chair; as usual she is wearing her white dress-coat. But droplets of sweat prickle her cheerless face. Her thin white lips are like death, and her large eyes are brimming with tears; they direct my gaze to the aquarium. Red Rebecca, open-eyed, is lying on her side, virtually encased in ice.

With a small hammer I freed the little body from the solid matter, and as I took out the goldfish Miss Fela burst into uncontrollable weeping. Rebecca was the only living thing she had. But there was nothing we could do, there is no antidote to death. Lucky little Rebecca — at least she died in her own bed. What a great privilege, in those surreal days, to outwit the ashes.

I kissed my teacher and left, just as the first star appeared and lit up heaven's callousness.

Perhaps three days later there was a knock on our door. Miss Fela had come to say goodbye. 'I finally received my wedding card,' she said, showing us her resettlement notice. 'At last I'll be the bride for once. Rumkowski has told me I'll be working in a kindergarten. Forgive me, good people, I must hurry. My children are waiting…'

≈ *Sparks in the Dark* ≈

Spring 1943. Europe's socialism was sinking into an abyss of iniquity, with the German and Austrian socialist parties fully integrated into the Nazi movement. Yet we Bundists in the ghetto of the waterless river had not begun to question our beliefs, not even when to our horror we learnt that the water-side workers in faraway New Zealand had gone on strike,

refusing (after their government had rejected their demands
for a pay rise) to load some armour destined for the war effort
against the Axis. We were hurt but did not judge — nothing
could shake our belief that the solidarity of the free world
would in the end prevail.

On May Day, I arrived at work earlier than usual and
secretly (so I thought) chalked a big zero on the daily pro-
duction-target board. I was denounced and summoned to the
office of the factory director, Kohen. 'Saboteur, saboteur!' he
yelled, shaking his fist into my face. 'I'll teach you!' Although
Kohen was also an officer in the ghetto police, he had recently
been warned by my co-workers that if he didn't control his
cruel excesses he would be taken care of. Kohen was a known
funk. I've heard somewhere that the rattlesnake is essentially
a coward, its rattle acting as a cover for its dread.

A day or so later, at around midnight, there was an alarm-
ing knock on our door, followed by the sound of a familiar
voice. It belonged to Motele Hoizer, my party's secret messenger. 'Hurry,' he urged, 'there's no time to lose, they're coming
to get you. Your parents must hide too; they're taking hos-
tages.'

Mother looked distraught. As we dressed, father remarked
to Motele: 'To find a hiding-place in a prison is like finding
sanity in an asylum, and we live in both.'

'Please,' Motele replied, 'there's no time for philosophy.
It's only for one night. We have received reliable information
that this is the last transport, for the time being.' And almost
at once he was off into the dark again, to return to his own
home.

Adjacent to our room lived a quiet eighteen-year-old student, Zev. His parents had been killed four years ago in an air-
raid, and his sick sister had been thrown out of a hospital
window into a waiting German truck for dispatch to the gas

chambers of Chelmno. Zev lived alone. We told him we would hide in the disused attic on the top floor of the building. 'Fine, just go!' he hissed. 'Run for your lives.'

Shortly afterwards we heard, from our attic hideout, the impudent clatter of police boots — and Zev's screams. 'I don't know where they are!' he cried. 'I don't know anything, and I'm not going, I'm not going!' The policemen gave him a merciless beating, but Zev stood his ground and they left empty-handed. A few minutes later he stumbled up the stairs and found us. He was bleeding all over. 'Don't come back yet,' he whispered. 'You don't know how cunning they are.'

For a while the four of us stood there together in the dark, hugging each other. Mother kissed Zev, and he cried. I don't think it was because of the beating. Zev was alone: he had no one to kiss him.

Next evening Motele brought news that the Russian armies on the eastern front were pressing their former ally hard, in Africa the Germans were in retreat, and there was serious talk about a second front in the west. The war was surely drawing to an end, yet this seemed to make little impression on the behaviour of the Kohens and their ilk — 'patricians of our circus state', as father put it, who still looked upon our puppet chairman with an air of reverence and admiration.

On the other hand, although our ghetto continued to be emptied of its Jews, we Bundists never lost faith in socialism — and in Schiller.

❧ The Merchant *in Ghetto* ❧

Kalman, the man I had befriended in the queue while waiting for our daily bread allocation, had come from a different town. He told me about the lively cultural life of his home ghetto, which had a small underground library, several reading circles and a semi-legal theatre condoned by the authorities. A particular event he related to me during one of our meetings has all the elements of legend, and maybe a legend is what it is. Yet there are few nobilities or cruelties in fiction that can equal the realities of my time. Here is Kalman's account, more or less as I remember it.

One dull Monday morning a black Mercedes made its way through the practically deserted ghetto streets, and pulled up softly in front of the theatre. The chauffeur jumped out smartly, swung open the rear door with gusto, and stood to attention as his superior, a man in his mid-fifties wearing a trim green-grey uniform, emerged from the car.

He was welcomed on the pavement by Moish Kawa, the stage director, who reverently bowed his head and led the German censor, Hans Hoffmann, to his tiny office. Depositing a parcel of food on the manuscript-cluttered desk, Hans, who was well aware of Moish's erudition, and of the irony of the bow, remarked: 'I like you, Moish. You are a compulsive communicator, like all good artists.'

'Thanks, Herr Hoffmann, but you give me too much credit,' the other replied. 'An artist-poet, more than any other person, has a responsibility to reflect justice and decency, and above all to oppose evil.'

'Quite so.'

'One of my teachers, the poet Broderzon, once delivered a lecture based on an old tale. A simple man was strolling with the prophet Elijah when he noticed in the distance a group of Jews passionately engrossed in prayer. "Tell me, Elijah," he asked, "will these men have a share in the world to come?" "No," the prophet replied. Further on, they spotted two strange figures with top-hats and colourful canes. "These two," said Elijah, "will be entitled to a share in the world to come — they are comedians, actors, entertainers. As such, they are bringers of hope, joy and laughter to a downcast humanity." That, my teacher concluded, is the ideal of true theatrical art.'

Hoffmann was smiling. 'You were blessed with a fine teacher, Moish. I agree wholeheartedly with his philosophy.'

'If that's the case,' said the director to the censor, who took an interest in Moish's family life, regularly bringing food and medicine for his family; 'if that's the case — and you know there is nothing personal in my question — then tell me, good sir, why are your people, who are so soaked in culture, in great theatre and poetry and sublime music, doing such unspeakable things to us?'

Hoffmann nodded sadly, then answered in a whisper, lest the very walls hear and betray him. 'Obedience is inherent in my people's makeup — obedience to authority, which one must not dare to question. And according to the teaching of that authority, your crime is your birth. Luther drummed it into our psyche. It is written in the sixteenth chapter of John, verse 6: *If a man abide not in me, he is cast forth as a branch, and withers; and men gather the branches, and throw them into the fire, and they are burned.*'

'I'm impressed. But how do *you* feel about that, Herr Hoffmann?'

'I think it's wrong, though I'm a devoted Christian... But I did not come today, my friend, to discuss religion. I've brought you a strict order from my superior, a playwright who thinks of himself as an artist of the first rank. He wants you to stage his version of *Der Kaufmann in Venedig*. He plans to invite many high dignitaries and military officials to the opening. You see, our playwright is convinced that the Jews bribed "that shopkeeper Shakespeare", as he puts it (our Führer says the English are a nation of shopkeepers), to insert a Jewish speech into the play. In order to right this wrong, he has rewritten some of Shylock's

lines.' Hoffmann pulled a manuscript from his briefcase and
quickly located the relevant page. 'Here we are.'

Moish read through the proposed changes to Shylock's
celebrated speech ('Hath not a Jew eyes?') in the third act.
After a prolonged silence, he said: 'My dear Herr Hoffmann,
to do this would be a betrayal of my lifelong belief in theatre,
and of the philosophy you so wholeheartedly endorsed just
now.'

The German fell back in his chair. 'You know what this
means, don't you? Your refusal could spell your end. And for
me... well, to fail at my age is not a very good affidavit for
one's future. Think what you are doing by refusing.'

But the director remained steadfast. Hoffmann left, never
to be seen again, and *The Merchant* was never staged in that
ghetto. Yet Moish Kawa, with his perceptive Semitic eyes,
miraculously made it through the war. He spent many years
searching for his benefactor, who was reputed to have once
been a superb Horatio in Max Reinhardt's *Hamlet*, at the
Deutsches Theater in Berlin in 1909. But all his searching
came to naught. Finally, it dawned on him that Hans Hoffmann was possibly none other than one of those strange
figures in Broderzon's tale, who, for carrying a spark of light
during a season of darkest despair, had doubtless been promoted to the domain of the world to come.

∾ *Vestibule* ∾

In the shadow of death, some people dream of bread while
others argue metaphysics.

Aron Wolman, one of my mentors in the ghetto, was a
man in his early forties, tiny of stature but deep of voice, with
a penetrating gaze. 'There are many ways of reading, of in-

terpreting our scripture, of musing upon our folklore,' he remarked one day, closing those gleaming eyes of his, perhaps to protect some inner vision. 'It is told that Abram smashed his father's clay idols to pieces, then placed the stick he had used into the hands of the oldest god. When asked by his angry father, Terah, "What have you done?", Abram answered: "It wasn't me, father — your chief god did this."'

Aron smiled, though hunger was reverberating in his stomach. (He ate only once a day, just a morsel of bread; the rest, whatever there was, he gave to his young teenage daughter, who was dying of tuberculosis.) 'Abram's deed,' he went on, 'can be seen as the first human rebellion against paganism, the first proclamation of the one and only invisible God... Invisibility!' his deep voice rang out emphatically. 'What a mighty contribution to a loftier monotheism—'

There was a sharp whistle, followed by shots, cries, a scream. '*Raus, raus, alle Juden!*' Abruptly, Aron's face was drained of all colour. But without losing his composure he switched off the light, walked towards the door and attached to it a note with a single word printed in red ink: *TYPHUS*. Then he came quietly back to his seat.

'What do I mean by "loftier monotheism"?' he resumed, as if the outside world was of no concern to him. 'One's inner freedom, one's inward sense of justice, one's total rejection of barbarism.' Moulding his words like a sculptor shapes his clay, Aron endowed each phrase with an almost physical presence. 'As I see it, such monotheism,' he concluded, 'is quintessentially anti-religious! It rejects not only all forms of xenophobia, but widens the boundaries of one's intellect, and one's spirituality.'

These words I heard more than sixty years ago, while enveloped in total darkness but for the searchlights journeying over our blind windowpane. I heard them from a weak

man of steel, in death's vestibule, who ate metaphysics instead
of bread.

∽ Mythology ∽

'Psychoanalysis,' said Aron Wolman, 'believes that the key to
any individual's character lies in the story of his or her childhood.' He had just begun his lecture, held in the home of one
of my friends, where we seven poets met once a fortnight.

To lend our meetings a festive hue, each of us would bring
a slice of bread taken from our weekly ration — for as it is
written, *Ein kemach, ein Torah* (without bread, no Torah). On
this occasion, the contribution of our host's mother was a hot
pot of chicory, plus a small dish of salt to dip the bread in.
Having prepared this sumptuous feast, she removed herself
from the premises, so as not to be tempted to appease with
even a solitary crumb her own hunger-racked stomach.

'Accordingly,' Wolman continued, 'the roots of the present
atrocities have their origins in the perpetrators' very mythology.
In the beginning, their legends tell us, was the giant Ymir. He
was the progenitor of all the terrible races that were to make the
world ring with bloody battles. At times these races were threatened by their own gods, who intended to exterminate them but
only saw them rise again, more numerous and stronger than
ever. The first god was Buri. Buri fathered Bor. One night, when
the moon did not permit Bor's offspring to sleep, they got up
and slaughtered their great-grandfather.

'But the gods were not content to have slain the giant —
obviously there was no respect for the dead. From Ymir's
blood they made the oceans, his flesh became the solid earth,
his bones the mountains and his teeth shingle. With his skull
they created the vault of heaven, with his brains the clouds,

and with his hair the trees.' Wolman paused. 'As you can see, my friends,' he stated with some emphasis, 'the marriage between murder and economy is not an accident, but rather the ancient principle of an everlasting mythological longing.'

At this point one of our group spoke up. 'Given our daily experience, it might appear that your argument from psycho-analysis is valid. But Aron, is it not true that our own mythology is also intertwined with murder, incest, fratricide, and many other brutalities?'

'Yes,' Aron replied. 'And yet, the mere fact that after four years of anguish, fear, starvation and hopelessness, hardly any murders have been committed in the ghetto, must tell us something.'

'And what is that?' asked a bushy-haired youth with a gleam in his eye.

'Perhaps something to do with our being in exile…'

'But all people are in exile, one way or another.'

'True, but the majority are not aware of it.'

'Do you mean to say that if we lost our awareness of exile, we would be capable of doing what *they* are doing?'

'Some things are the more powerful for being beyond simple explanations,' Aron retorted. Then, betraying an agitation that bordered on anger, he sank his teeth into the last sliver of bread, threw his worn-out coat over his scrawny shoulders, and departed.

⮞ *Why We Didn't Rise* ⮜

The last confrontation I had with my party leader, Israel Binenberg, took place a world ago, yet every detail of that encounter, even the most trifling, is still vividly alive in the chamber of my memories.

We met in his flat and sat facing each other across his table, I the member of an unarmed cell of the ghetto underground, and he my political instructor. Israel was a small, stocky, well-built man, a carpenter by trade, with a moon face and foxy, mocking eyes. Although he had a rather nasal voice, he could colour it with both severity and irony, and he could galvanize a crowd like few others. Sitting opposite me now, clad in a blue shirt whose rolled-back sleeves nearly covered his strong arms, he kept adjusting the table-lamp with his short fingers, the better to scrutinize my face from the shadows in which he had securely planted himself.

'What on earth has become of us,' I asked, 'that we, the heirs of a great revolutionary tradition, should take all this lying down?'

Israel surveyed me impassively before replying in a voice wooden with gravity: 'And with what arms, my great revolutionary, would you propose to stage our rebellion? Do you know that in our armoury, which is guarded by our faithful comrade Kusznierski, there sleeps peacefully one solitary gun, no better than a toy? And have you forgotten that not only are we encircled by barbed wire, but also, beyond, by an ocean of hostility?'

If I was taken aback, it did not prevent me from pressing ahead. 'Well, you're the leader,' I retorted, my audacity mounting. 'Wasn't it your responsibility to think of this when there was still time?'

'Hold it, hold it, brave Jacobin!' Israel's voice was suddenly alive with authority and reproach. 'We are living in an age when no leadership is answerable to its followers. We do what we think is right, for the whole community. The same rule governs the Zionists in ghetto, and even the ever-volatile Communists' activities.' He was arguing with incontestable clarity.

But I was bent on a different logic. 'Look, our youth is ready to fight, and we *will* fight. We have a plan. First of all, at a time to be determined, groups of five will attack sentries throughout the ghetto and quickly deprive them of their weapons. We calculate that within ten minutes we may have as many as fifty guns in our hands…'

Israel was now visibly alarmed. Indignantly he lit a cigarette and, fanning the smoke away with his short arm, burst forth with a vehemence I had never before witnessed. 'Don't you dare!' he exclaimed. 'We will expel all mad hotheads from the party.' Then, withdrawing even deeper into the shadows, so that I could hear but not see him, he changed his tactic. He stretched his hand towards a drawer and opened it. For the first time after all the years of my ghetto life, I saw a whole loaf of bread and a sizeable hunk of juicy white cheese. Miracles like this appeared only in homes closely connected with the higher echelons of the pyramid.

Israel motioned for me to help myself. 'You know,' he said, calm and reflective now, while I cut a thin slice of bread, broke off a small lump of cheese and sat back to savour this unexpected bounty, 'I've coined a new maxim; it might just help our people more than guns. *Live and outlive* — I mean, of course, outlive *them*, our oppressors.'

'Very nice. Very ingenious.' In no time I had gulped down my little feast. 'You've just defeated our last hope of making a stand.'

'Well, dear comrade, *a living dog is better than a dead lion.*'

'That was all very well for King Solomon, but I can hardly see how it applies to *our* hopeless situation…'

It was long past curfew. Going home was a perilous experience, and in the dark a sentry's boots always sounded ominous. The moon I had once trusted had lately volunteered

her services to the devils; she was brighter than ever, and I was
convinced she had overheard my plans and would soon pass
them on to the enemy. Look! Was her black streetwalker's eye
not beckoning to her new lover, the soldier?...

My parents were already in bed — the ghetto way of combating hunger and a total absence of fuel. 'Where were you?'
my mother asked nervously. I told them the truth; after all,
they were both longstanding members of the party. Mother at
once sided with Israel. I turned for support to father, the
oldest revolutionary in town. All he said, to my astonishment,
was: 'One difficult day of life is worth a hundred years of
glorious death.' I turned off the light.

Lying in bed, allowing my eyes to journey the windowpane, I took note of how the night, with her long dark hands,
stacked black boulder upon black boulder until there were no
more stars to be seen.

❧ The Law at Work ❧

Ours was a neighbourhood of slender people, but slender not
through any inclination to diet. 'Hunger' was, to us, a household word. Even so, one should not try to compare our prewar
hunger to the starvation that assailed us during the ghetto
years. Ghetto famine was beyond the imagination even of a
Knut Hamsun.

A family might go to bed at night and wake up in their very
own private morgue. At the height of our suffering, we died at
the rate of some forty people a day. And yet, though it may
appear unreal, our ghetto also contained a well-fed elite for
whom 'shortage' was an alien concept — an elite who had ser-
vants and lived in proper houses, surrounded by little gardens
where the air smelt of raisins and almonds and fresh green grass.

The Blums were new neighbours, a family of four: he was a coachman, she a cleaning lady, and they had a small boy and a smaller girl. When Mr Blum was reported missing in action defending our country, his wife was left to fend for the children on her own. She was always the first in the queue to collect her weekly food-rations, and in the evenings she would come over to tell my mother of her joy in being able to feed her little ones. 'The war will soon be over,' she would say, 'and my husband will come back to me. I'll show him his kids, and he'll take me in his arms and say, *Thank you, my love, you have done well.*'

It was a black day when Mrs Blum's weekly provisions were stolen. 'Murderers!' she cried. 'Murderers! What have you done? You've slaughtered my children! What am I to do? Oh God, what am I to do?'

She could do nothing. Ghetto life knew very few mercies.

A week later, when my mother went up to the attic to hang up some washing, she found two orange enamel saucepans lying on the floor. Assuming that they belonged to someone who had been 'resettled', she took them home, and the same evening used them to cook some soup for dinner. Just as she was about to serve our lavish meal, Mrs Blum burst in, looked around and left without a word. Half an hour later she returned in the company of her cousin, a member of the Jüdischer Ordnungsdienst, the Jewish ghetto police. Pointing to mother's new acquisitions, she exclaimed: 'In those I kept my children's food!'

I was arrested on the spot. At the watchhouse they asked me to sign a statement admitting my crime. When I refused I was tied up; then, after fifteen minutes of solid thrashing, one of my tormentors showed me the dotted line on a sheet of paper. 'We'll make you sign, sonny,' he said. 'No!' I replied, observing his grotesque pretence at Polish, his uneasy self-assurance and his absurdly affected manner of speaking.

In the morning I was set free. When I got home, father told me they had come to see him and had informed him that I had signed a confession. He didn't believe them, but was ready to hand over every scrap of food we had in return for his son's release. They had agreed — on condition that Mr Blum's shoes, which had been stolen along with the food, be included. Father took off his only pair and offered it to them.

But these were not the shoes in question, so they had left empty-handed.

What had happened was this: Father had gone to see my parents' employer for the past thirty-five years, Pinkus Gerszowski, who belonged to the ghetto hierarchy. Gerszowski had contacted the director of the factory where I worked, who confirmed my presence at work on the day of Mrs Blum's tragedy.

A fortnight later Mrs Blum's provisions were stolen again. She grew suicidal and would not stop screaming. 'What will my husband say? What will he say? Tell me, good people, what am I to do?' Somehow, with the help of her neighbours, she made it through to the next weekly ration.

Shortly afterwards, on a grey Monday morning when Mrs Blum had gone to work leaving her two little ones with a friend, someone stood at her door and tampered with the lock. Softly humming to himself, the thief entered, gathered into a small sack what remained of the family's food, and was about to leave when Mrs Blum's policeman cousin jumped out from the cupboard and knocked over the intruder — whom he immediately recognized as a young tough living in our block. 'You'll rot in jail for the rest of your life,' he told him, and escorted him to the watchhouse. By dinnertime, however, our thief was back in the yard.

How was that possible?

Simple. His uncle happened to be the Mrs Blum's cousin's superior!

❧ *Honeymoon* ❧

Żabia 13 had once been a school of three hundred children.
The Germans evicted them all, burned their books and replaced the benches with sewing-machines. Our working day
began at eight and finished at six, with thirty minutes for
lunch; every second Sunday we had off. The director of our
factory, the police officer Kohen, was known for his cruelty
and stupidity. He would lash workers with his leather belt and
shower them with obscenities for downing tools five minutes
before knock-off time.

In 1902 a Bundist cobbler and activist, Hirsh Lekert, had
attempted to assassinate the governor of Vilna, Von Wahl, for
doing exactly what Kohen was doing. Lekert died for this
endeavour, but lived on as a legend in the hearts of his comrades. Our place, however, had no Lekerts.

The factory was set up in such a manner that no worker
would be face to face with another. Twenty-year-old Adamowicz,
known as Adam for short, sat in front of me. A tall, emaciated
and likeable fellow, whose features would be paradise for any
cartoonist, he was a frightful cynic about the holiest things in
life, though not on the subject of food. Hunger made Adam
cry.

Come twelve o'clock he would grow restless, almost wildly
so. 'Soup time, soup time,' he kept repeating in his deep
baritone, and when he heard the steel barrel of steamy liquid
being rolled into the factory yard, his already protruding ears
pricked up, his narrow eyes lit up, and the nostrils of his over-
sized nose (which occupied most of his meagre face) became
alive with an animal awareness. As usual, his excitement was
shortlived: in vain did he search in his bowl for a chunk of
potato — the thick part of the meal which our forty-year-old
server, Maryla, reserved for Kohen and his associates.

I recall the fateful day when Adam changed his tactics. Instead of being first in the queue to obtain a serving of Maryla's mercy, he placed himself last. An unreachable treasure lay at the bottom of the barrel and he was determined to secure his share. Almost dancing with anticipation as he edged closer, Adam, his deep baritone in excellent form, assailed Maryla with the ditty of a well-known ghetto poet:

> *O lady with the ladle,*
> *I don't mean to bicker,*
> *But please, a little deeper,*
> *Please, a little thicker…*

Within a few days Adam's bowl was being rewarded with twice its usual portion, and soon afterwards he told me that he was going to marry Maryla. Why, I enquired. 'That dowry of hers, of course — and love, love,' he replied. 'At midday a pot of thick soup, at midnight a thick pot of flesh!'

The 'wedding', if it took place, must have been a low-key affair. Maryla's husband was presumed to have died somewhere in the snowfields of Russia, Adam had no siblings, and his deeply religious parents had been resettled to heaven the previous year. But news of the happy match quickly reached our all-knowing Kohen, and since his soup was no longer quite what it used to be, he decided to take remedial action. When Adam, who had always been one of the best workers in our group, received his next pay, he found to his astonishment a note advising of his impending resettlement. A similar note was inserted into Maryla's pay. The following day Adam came to work to say goodbye. I asked him where he was going. 'Honeymoon,' he said, and vanished.

When he reached his destination, they made him write a letter:

Dear friends,

We arrived safely, the journey was a breeze. Maryla was immediately appointed manageress in a fancy kitchen. As you can see, the dowry holds fast! And before long I'll be meeting up with my dear parents.

Yours, Adam

A Reading

Our literary meetings stood out for me like a cultural ark in the time of an anti-cultural flood. Some readers may see this as a post-ghetto illusion, for truly, how can one think of culture with death constantly knocking on the door? And yet, anyone who ever did time will know that even in prison it is possible to experience a sense of freedom. Sometimes, hope can be strongest when lying on its deathbed.

My colleagues, like myself, had not been brought up on the Bible, so the piece we were about to hear on this occasion came as something of a novelty. 'A genuine story, and especially a fable,' began our reader for that evening (sadly, I'm unable to recall his name), 'travels the oceans of time only to return to its port of departure. My story tonight is called *Chosen*. One could say that it is about the past, the present, and the future...'

When we had settled into a unanimous readiness, he unfolded a sheet of paper from his pocket and commenced his reading. It is not an altogether unfamiliar tale, and I'll reconstruct it here as best I can.

God almighty was sitting on cloud nine with His angels one day when, out of the blue (or was it the black?) there appeared his highness, the Adversary. 'And where have you been, my boy?' God asked him.

'I have been roaming Your world, Master,' the other replied.

God nodded. 'Did you happen to catch sight of My chosen? Surely there is no other community on earth like theirs — blameless, upright, charitable, their synagogues always packed, and not just on the holy Sabbath.'

'Ah, well, Sir,' sneered the Adversary, 'they have good reason to be as they are. You provided that tribe of cobblers, tailors, joiners, weavers and little rabbis with the best of life. As it is written, *Happy is the man who is satisfied with his lot.* But try to deprive them of Your benevolence, and You'll soon find out what a miserable crowd they really are.'

'You think so?' said God. 'Let's wager on it — I leave them in your hands.'

So the Adversary darted back to hell, picked up his most monotonous accomplice, dull as a dirty autumn fog but more vicious than a crazy dog, and told him: 'Take care of these so-called *chosen* for me.' The diligent delegate quickly set to work. First he deprived the people in question of their livelihood, looted their homes, stole their possessions, burned down their prayer-houses, saw to it that they received pitiless beatings. Yet the community remained steadfast. 'God has given, and God has taken away,' they said as one. 'May His name be blessed for ever and ever.'

Before long the Adversary presented himself in heaven. 'Well, what do you say now?' remarked the Almighty with some satisfaction. 'Have you noticed my people's fidelity, their resolute integrity in the face of suffering and hardship?'

The Adversary was quick to respond. 'Sir, let me probe them deeper,' he urged, 'and You'll soon get a taste of their wicked, blasphemous nature.'

'They are in your hands,' said God with a confident smile.

So the Adversary incited his humourless offsider to herd God's chosen into ghettos, and he appointed cruel taskmasters who tortured the people and worked them to death. Yet still the members of the condemned community stood fast. 'Should we accept only good from God,' they cried in unison, 'and reject all pain, misfortune and evil?'

Suspecting at last that he could not make these stiff-necked Jews turn against their Almighty after all, the Adversary angrily summoned his unhappy henchman once more. 'Make soap of them,' he commanded, 'and let them vanish into thin air like bubbles on a windy day.'

When the people learnt of their impending fate, they gathered in what was left of their little houses, rent their clothes, and with ash on their heads chanted:

Perish the day when we were chosen,
and the night it was announced
that a holy nation had been conceived!

…And God, on hearing such terrible words (our reader concluded), will *break down*, and will utter a heart-wrenching *lament*, and will be ready to *resign* from His heavenly seat. But to His great amazement, the remnant of this wretched, ill-treated people can not, *will* not, accept His resignation. Falling on their faces, they will implore him: 'O Lord, master of the universe, do not abandon us. Don't leave us completely alone in a world gone mad.'

≈ *Yiddish Lullaby* ≈

What a marvellous mother she was. Even those who despised her had to admit it. And if one had the privilege of looking into her large dark eyes, one was reminded of God's light. I last saw her sitting on the shore of a silent lake, enveloped in sunset while it was still day. She sat beneath a willow tree, humming 'Raisins and Almonds', dreaming her bygone bliss and then, with trembling lips, the song of her life — which I understood so well because it was also mine:

By the lake stands a tree
The tree of a thousand sighs;
On the tree sits a bird
With sad, storytelling eyes.

Suddenly we heard footsteps, a phantom braving the dark. His voice, like bowstrokes on a violin, resounded in the dusk. 'How close to my heart is your song,' he cried. 'How close, wise minstrel. When you sing I hear the breeze rustle the desert sands, the song of Miriam, the steps of our forefathers walking into eternity, the murmur of the letters, the whisper of time itself.'

She turned towards the voice. 'Then come to me, prince of the golden verse. I am tired, and my lids are like lead. Come, tuck your mother in, for old times' sake, and cradle her to sleep with your half-forgotten lullaby.'

And so he did. 'There was once a king,' he began. 'His queen had a garden, and the garden a tree, and the tree a nest, and the nest a little bird I loved. *Aili lili-lu, aili lili-lu.* Then came the wind and destroyed the nest and broke the little bird's wings. I have no home in the east, no home in the west. *Aili lili-lu, aili lili-lu.*'

As she closed her eyes I heard her say: 'And I have no more fears but one. A time is coming when a famine will descend upon the land. Not hunger for bread, not thirst for water, but hunger and thirst for the hearing of a Yiddish word. And men shall wander from sea to sea, to seek the word, but they shall not find it…'

❧ *Ghetto Poets* ❧

We were six young men and one young woman. She and I would cuddle and kiss and caress, but we never actually 'did it'. A tiny girl with dark squinting eyes, she had a seductive smile and thin, gentle, beckoning hands. For a whole year we met in her home, a small room where she lived with her sister, who had an infant girl born out of wedlock. My sweetheart would describe how, night by night, her sister and her lover would tear at each other's flesh. 'I wish *we* could go all the way,' she said, 'instead of just fondling each other.'

'Have you thought of what might happen if we did?' I reminded her.

'I don't care. We're just outsiders looking in. Why *shouldn't* we live for today?'

I felt she was right yet I couldn't bring myself to go along. Apart from anything else, I was inhibited by the presence of the child, who was looked after by my girlfriend during the daytime when her sister was working. Eventually, after a silly but rowdy altercation, we parted company.

A few days later, at a poetry reading under the guidance of our learned Aron Wolman, we met again. These sessions always took place in the modest home of one of my friends, a single room divided by a curtain, creating the illusion of a double apartment. I remember every stick of furniture in that flat. On the right as you entered stood an unlit stove, and on the left a large brown cupboard, to which the curtain was attached; the cupboard housed a collection of blue-bound books by Anatole France, among them the famous *Penguin Island* and *Thaïs*, which had been borrowed and read by all of us. In the centre of the room was the lame table around which we sat together. I liked my friend's home, and I liked his quiet mother — who seemed to have stepped straight out of a story by Gorky. After we consumed the bit of dry bread each of us had brought, which for most of us was our daily meal, it was time for Wolman's talk.

'One might wonder,' he began, 'why on earth, in the current political climate, one should bother about the Polish–Jewish literary "osmosis". Or, is it *precisely* because of our present situation that people like us are compelled to examine our literary partnership — if only in order not to be consumed by the hatred that surrounds us?'

Wolman then briefly surveyed some of the important Jewish writers and their contribution to Polish literature: the work of Julian Tuwim, Bolesław Leśmian, Mieczysław Jastrum, Marian Hemar, Józef Wittlin, and of course the tragic Bruno Schultz. From here he deftly turned to I. L. Peretz, the great Yiddish writer who had proclaimed that foreign ideas plant foreign cultures — though this did not mean, Aron stressed, that we had to lock ourselves up in a cultural ghetto. 'On the contrary, Peretz argued that cultural isolation led to spiritual death. We have to take and give, share each other's spiritual heritage, yet remain Jewish. Remember,' Wolman added; 'a writer who forsakes his roots has no place in posterity.'

He then spoke at length about the poet Adam Mickiewicz, and about the hunchback Jew Yankel the musician in his *Pan Tadeusz* — one of the great Polish literary masterpieces of all time — and went on to analyse the Polish influence on our Jewish writing, in particular that of *Wesele* by Stanisław Wyspiański (another exalted Polish poet) on Peretz's play *At Night at the Old Market*. Wolman also read out a poem which the Yiddish master had dedicated to his beloved Polish poet, Maria Konopnicka:

> *I saw poems white as snow*
> *blossoming fragrantly as in spring*
> *and pure as the bluest sky at night,*

and like a sad angel in thought
they sang of love…

After this, each of us read a piece — most of them about
our disrupted lives, our aborted youth, our sadness, but few
without a ray of hope or a longing for universal peace and
redemption. The last to read was my no-longer girlfriend. I
cannot recall the exact form of her poem, but the message at
its heart is lodged in my memory:

A ghetto might tarnish the nobility of young love,
but to erase it completely is to succumb to cowardice.

The moment she finished her poem she ran from the room
as if it was burning. I gave chase, flying recklessly down the
three flights of stairs, and caught up with her on the bottom,
street-level landing. I pulled her to me and tried to kiss her
tears away. 'Don't!' she almost shouted, tearing herself away.
'There's no need to pretend — we're not on the stage!' And she
hurried off sobbing into the night.

❧ *Enigmas* ❧

Future scholars of the social sciences will shake their heads in
disbelief. How was it possible, they will ask, for so many of
these permanently hungry ghetto-dwellers, whose only release
from their miseries was death (a death which arrived daily), to
continue to immerse themselves in writing poetry, studying
languages, engaging in philosophical discourse, and conduct-
ing heated debates over purely intellectual abstractions?
    Once, while in the ghetto, I had the good fortune to spend
time with a group of former yeshiva students, twenty-odd years

my seniors, to whom the Yiddish language had opened the
gates to European literature and had transformed these people
into a formidable intellectual elite, flag-bearers in the republic
of words, with a hatred of all dictatorial systems. No wonder
our overlords saw them as enemies of the state.

'Perhaps,' one of the group remarked, 'our mistake is that
we forever consider ourselves *citizens*, whereas the people we
alive amongst think of us merely as *sojourners*. Look, for fifteen
hundred years we lived in Spain,' he argued, warming up. 'We
settled on the Iberian Peninsula when it was still a waste and
desolate land, we invested our blood, our sweat and our intellect in its future, yet in the end we were made to leave. And now?
We have dwelt in this country for over a thousand years, and
helped to build it, and we're still considered intruders by our
neighbours.'

'But do you know why?' asked another, and proceeded to
answer his own question. 'Perhaps our crime is, on the one
hand, that we are constantly seeking shelter with xenophobic
rulers disliked by the masses; and on the other, that we inject
into the insularity of our neighbours the dream of a universal
brotherhood, which antagonizes those rulers — who conveniently rob us by exiling us from their land.'

'Though wouldn't you think,' commented a third, 'that it is
our wanderings which forged the very essence of what we are?'

'And what might that essence be?'

'Intellectual acumen.'

'And yet, according to Rashi, wandering has three effects:
it breaks up one's family life, reduces one's wealth, and lessens
one's standing in the world.'

'Precisely so,' said a man we all called Trotsky, not for his
political hue but on account of his goatee. At heart a poet
trapped between the present and the past, Trotsky was a real
charmer. The only thing I resented about him was his slow,

condescending smile. 'It seems to me that you all lack passion for the land that our faith should have ingrained in our psyche,' he went on. 'The land where we can all be regarded as legitimate settlers…'

'Nothing will change,' someone interrupted him. 'Do you really believe that after two thousand years of wandering we can transform ourselves into settlers?'

'*Vil nor…*' retorted Trotsky. 'If you but so desire it.'

Gazing up at the firmament, he continued: 'It's only just past midday and our mighty God has already dipped his brush in the blood of our martyrs.' Then, out of the blue, he launched into a Yiddish verse by Yosef Papiernikov:

> *Maybe I build my castles in the air,*
> *Maybe the story of God isn't true;*
> *In my dreams it's better, in my dreams it's brighter,*
> *In my dreams the sky is bluer than blue.*

As he made for the door, Trotsky pulled up his jacket collar, turned his head towards us and, with his condescending little smile, announced: 'It seems to me that all our intellectualizing may have led us to the brink of an unavoidable abyss. At a time like this, gentlemen, an ounce of common sense might be better than a ton of scholarship.'

For some reason, we laughed as we waved him off.

∾ *Purim* ∾

It was ghetto life which brought about the democratization of sorrow in our tenement. David Klinger, a refined well-educated man, lost his wife to a sudden selection; three months later his unlearned neighbour Rachel, ten years his senior, was cradling

him to sleep every night. David's political enemy Velvele, nick-
named *Sheker* (lie), who believed that V. I. Lenin was King Solomon incarnate, walked around our yard after the Soviets' successful spring offensive, singing, in Yiddish-accented German:

> *Auf, auf zum Kampf, zum Kampf!*
> *Zum Kampf sind wir geboren!*
> *Dem Karl Liebknecht haben wir's geschworen,*
> *Dem Rosa Luxemburg reichen wir die Hand.*

Velvele said that David strutted about like a national hero
but was in truth a coward afraid to sleep in the dark by himself.

'Unfortunately,' David would retort, 'misery acquaints a
person with strange bedfellows. This life we lead has no prece-
dent. Whether we like it or not, we are being terrorized daily
by loneliness.' And perhaps to aggravate Velvele, he might
add: 'As far as I can see, without a national homeland our
whole Jewish existence will have been one frightful mistake.'

David Klinger was a fine fellow, a wonderful idealist, and
a Zionist who belonged to the extreme wing of that movement. Joseph Trumpeldor, killed in 1920 defending the Tel
Hai settlement in Palestine, was to David a legendary hero,
while the name of Jabotinsky he uttered like a psalm.

Even in the most adverse circumstances, David would uphold the Jewish national tradition — if only verbally. I recall a
visit he paid us one cold and cheerless evening. After a word or
two about the political situation he mentioned Purim, and all
at once, as if entering a trance, David the dreamer was on a hike
into history. There, he eyed the foolish king Ahasuerus (also
known as Xerxes), and then his malevolent chief minister, the
former barber and bath-attendant Haman; and when the beautiful queen Esther made an appearance David's face lit up.

Arm in arm with Mordechai the Just, who brought to naught Haman's deceitful machinations against the Jews, he would lead our people into a free Palestine under the triumphant flutter of blue-and-white banners…

So hallucinated our idealist friend on that howling evening of 9 March 1943. The morrow would bring Purim, commemorated by the Jews as well as the Germans: the Jews celebrated Haman's demise twenty-four centuries ago, the Germans his present and glorious rebirth.

In the gallery of my memories there hangs a picture covered with rag-years and framed in white snow. It shows a morning in fog, and hundreds of wooden clogs shod with slush, tramping across a timber footbridge, and in the background stands a gallows, where, from nine ropes and with mouths open, ten Jews are dangling (for one of the ropes is shared by a father and son), on their faces a few meek and dying rays of sun, and around them six men in black rejoicing at Haman's resurrection. The picture is dated 'Wednesday, 10 March 1943'. Time has almost erased the painter's name.

≈ *Anniversary* ≈

The closeness of the Jewish family unit was something of which our arch-adversary was all too aware, and its final destruction was his obsession. Maybe this stemmed from the fact that his father had been born out of wedlock. In any case, he set out on a course of effectively starving his victims to death, doubtless in the belief that we would soon be eating each other's flesh…

At the start of every week we would collect our weekly bread rations. My mother took out her innocent scales, her indifferent knife, and cut the bread into three equal parts. (My two sisters, each with her little girl, lived apart from us, though in the same tenement block.) Mother made sure that we had enough for just one slice each per morning, so that the loaf would last through the week. But on one occasion father transgressed, secretly helping himself to some of mother's portion. Mother was horrified when she discovered this, and recalled her friend Berenice's anguish over her own Josef's lapse. But she responded by giving father the rest of her bread. 'He needs it more than I do,' she said. 'He is weaker, and he's only human.'

My parents had been married on 25 December 1913, and this was a date we celebrated even in the darkest moments of our family life. I recall our last such celebration, their thirtieth anniversary, in the winter of 1943-44, when the walls of our unheated room wore a brilliant coat of frost. I never learnt where my sisters had got hold of the two brown candles they brought over – I thought the colour was a bad omen. Meanwhile, however, there was a cake baked from chaff and another from potato-peels, and mother boiled up a special brew of water.

We ate and drank. Then, as he did every year, father took out the old letter – yellowed from spending its life between the pages of an ancient book – and the three desiccated twigs that had once been abloom with three glorious white roses, and he read out, as he did every year, the words he had written to his bride on their wedding night.

When he came to the line 'I'll be true to you, my love, for the rest of my days', his tongue stumbled, his face broke, and suddenly father was sobbing. I had never seen him cry. My two sisters were aghast, they didn't know what had happened. But mother and I knew. That transgression of a few months ago weighed heavily upon him, he still couldn't forgive himself. I'll never forget the way mother got up and embraced him. 'You are my husband,' I heard her whisper. 'You're my husband.'

❧ *Confession* ❧

It is early April 1944. The winter is almost gone but, here and there, clusters of snow are still rusting away what remains of their white lives. The forenoons are still freezing, and up above, on the unblemished blue expanse, the sun like a golden iceberg is eyeing the discontented day tottering on the cross-roads of the seasons.

It's Sunday morning. My father in his sheepskin coat gazes into the stove, where our last picture-frame is fighting the flames for its wooden life. He looks resigned, he is not well, plagued by a severe inflammation of his joints, and the only remedy is fatty food and Vigantol, both of them available only to those who are part of, or connected to, the higher levels of the ghetto pyramid.

He beckons me over and, without preliminaries, begins. 'My existence has become a bitter drink,' he says, 'yet I must swallow it day by day, drop by drop, until there is no more liquid in the flask.' Thus speaks my father, the eternal doubter, at this moment uncharacteristically firm. 'We know there are strong rumours,' he goes on, 'of a final ghetto liquidation, and as your mother once said, if any of us will make it, it must be you, the strongest and the youngest in the family.'

'No, dad!'

'Please, son, don't interrupt. Perhaps I'm telling you this because I have a need to talk, to talk at a time when our lives hang between a yes and a no. My father — your grandfather Yeruchim — was a melamed, a teacher, a fanatically religious man. My mother, Perl Gittel, was a housewife, and I a yeshiva student. We were very poor people, but my father believed that it was God's will. I rebelled against such a God, I refused to serve a cruel God, and joined the revolutionary Bund. In 1907 I was arrested. My mother came to visit me and, seeing her son behind bars, suffered a heart attack and died. I have never forgiven myself. After I was freed I went to see my father but he wouldn't look at me.'

He stopped, as if to gasp for a breath of air before continuing.

'I threw myself into socialist activities, into party life, hoping to build a just world without poverty, but my mother's image never left me, never, never. Now, thinking back, I'm sure I was exactly like my father, a zealot, only on a different landscape. Bundist theory became my Torah, the red flag my prayer-shawl. Now, all this has lost its meaning. This war, like the previous one, has miserably betrayed socialism, and this ghetto has transformed our once glorious party brotherhood into a soup-kitchen idealism. I am not blaming anyone. Humanity and decency are the first victims of hunger. When the ghetto was set up, a group of my comrades formed themselves into a self-appointed council; it was the only way we could reorganize the party and mobilize the membership. They approached me to head a delegation of textile workers (I had been one of their leaders, and for twenty years their elected judge), a delegation to Chaim Rumkowski, who had just been appointed by the Germans as Eldest of the Jews. The Germans knew precisely whom to choose when they usurped our town. I told my colleagues that to negotiate with this character was to succumb to his demands or bribes, so they picked somebody else. What happened I don't know, because their dealings took place behind closed doors.'

Here father paused again. I had the impression that he was chewing over what he had just told me — perhaps he had said too much. This man, who had seen in the Bund the ideal latter-day expression of the prophets, this God-intoxicated agnostic, had always been cautious with words. He was not one to needlessly condemn or praise: nothing gets better for being condemned, he would say, nothing gets better for being praised.

'Son, all this reminds me of a passage I once read in Søren Kierkegaard's book, *Either/Or*. A fire broke out backstage in a theatre, and the clown came out to inform the audience. They thought it was a joke and applauded. He repeated his warning, but they cheered even more loudly. Kierkegaard supposed that this was how the world would be destroyed — amid general applause from all the wits who believed it was a joke…'

Father fell silent and I knew he was already somewhere else. He was a master at being absent when the need came upon him. Turning his face away without another word, he fixed his stoical gaze on the embers dying in the stove.

❧ *The Logic of Water* ❧

Sickly sixty-year-old Szymon Brener, known in our little world for his intrusiveness and his crude loquacity — who, thanks to his son's diligence in the ghetto police, had evaded, along with his wife, many roundups and resettlements — invited himself into our apartment a week before the rumours of the total liquidation of our ghetto became a reality.

When Szymon opened our door, father was making some notes on a few pieces of paper. 'Panie Gershon,' he shouted excitedly, 'have you been keeping a diary?'

'Sort of,' father replied.

'Can I have a peep?'

'No, Szymon, you can't.'

'Why not?'

'It's private.'

'So at least tell me what you're writing about.'

Father maintained his customary calm. 'It's about memory,' he said.

'Memory?'

'Yes — the liar's greatest enemy.'

Not knowing quite how to take this little conundrum, our visitor smiled foolishly and plunged ahead regardless.

'Panie Gershon, they're talking about a complete liquidation of our ghetto, but don't believe them. You know, Panie Gershon,' and his voice assumed an authoritative tone, 'my son has first-hand information. Sure, some of us will have to go — maybe fifteen thousand, thirty thousand, perhaps even fifty thousand, who knows? But just like on the previous occasions, our Rumkowski will outsmart the Germans, and at the end of the war he'll march victorious out of the ghetto, ahead of all the people he saved. You know, Panie Gershon, there's a chapter in the Talmud which actually legitimizes our Eldest's strategy.' And without stopping, Szymon launched into his Talmudic commentary.

'Two men are travelling in the desert. One of them has a flask of water. If they both drink from the flask, neither will survive the journey, as there isn't enough water to sustain them both before they reach the next settlement. However, if only one of them drinks, he will be able to reach the settlement. Concerning this problem, Ben Petura held that it is better that both should drink and die, than that one of them should see the death of his fellow traveller. This teaching was accepted until Rabbi Akiva came along and invoked the Torah, where it is written that "your brother may live with you" — implying, he argued, that your own life took precedence and there was no obligation for a person to save another's life at the expense of his own. Thus the owner of the flask should use all the water to ensure his own survival…'

I looked at father and knew that he was about to explode. Yet somehow he harnessed his rage. 'Do you know, Szymon, what you've just said?' His voice was slow and controlled. 'Do you know?' he repeated, the anger beginning to show. 'To equate

Rabbi Akiva's sense of justice and respect for life with Rumkowski's logic is, in my opinion, an unforgivable obscenity.'

'But why, why?' cried the other, taken aback.

'First of all,' said father, regaining his composure, 'the
Talmud talks of *two* people, and only one of them has a flask
of water, and it's his right to decide to drink and live. But here,
there was once a community of a hundred and seventy thousand souls, and from the very inception of our confinement
— of our desert journey, if you like — not I and not you, but
only this so-called Eldest has held in his hands the flask of
water, and he, this miserable clown, has adjudicated — in the
interests of our enemy — who is to drink and who is not. And
let me reiterate, Szymon: only a fool could employ the Talmud
to justify Rumkowski's madness.'

At this point mother gave her husband a stern look, as if
to say 'Be careful'. But my worn-out dad, who I think had
already made peace with eternity, took no notice. Perhaps his
intuition told him it would make no difference. So he persisted.

'Look here, Szymon, I cannot tell you how I would feel in
such a dilemma. But I can assure you that all those Jews who
have a God in their soul and eventually march out of this
ghetto alive, knowing that someone else died in their place, will
walk the earth for the rest of their days with a heavy heart.'

≈ *Dream* ≈

I arrived in spring and stood at a crossroads near the ghetto.

The countryside was already in bloom; the grass was a lush
young green, sprinkled with brilliant yellow wildflowers. From
nearby I could hear the silvery tinkle of my homely little rivulet,
and the friendly greetings of birches, as I emerged from the

Yiddish-speaking forest and set off along the Black Road that led to the village. I stopped for a moment beneath a royal oak, from which was suspended a huge crucifix bearing a shadowy figure. Before I could look more closely, I noticed in the distance my old friend Jaś. 'Hey Jaś,' I cried, 'it's me! Remember how we used to roast potatoes at sunset in the open field?' But Jaś wouldn't answer, and when I tried to take a step in his direction the road between us expanded, expanded, as if by magic, and kept expanding until Jaś vanished. So I started to walk towards the place where I had once spent my summer holidays, and on the way I passed by the old redbrick villa I remembered. On its veranda, just like years ago, two young girls in white dresses, holding each other around the waist, danced relentlessly to a tango coming from their tarnished gramophone.

Finally I came to the farmhouse where we used to rent a room during our vacations. The war had changed nothing here. Across from the humble farmer's cottage, its windows adorned with gaily-coloured flowerpots, a herd of black-and-white cows grazed peacefully. Rex, who had known me well, was lazing in front of his kennel, with flies buzzing about his eyes, and in the endless blue sky a white stork was searching for its nest, blown away by the autumn wind.

Quite unexpectedly, Kazia appeared. It was five years since we had made love here; she had been fifteen then, but it was a young woman who now walked towards me with open out-stretched arms, her head adorned with a wreath of corn-flowers which matched her deep-set blue eyes and her golden hair lifting in the breeze. 'What are you doing here?' I asked.

'I knew you were coming,' she replied. 'I've been so feverish lately — come, let me share my fever with you.'

We sneaked into the barn, where the breath of a peaceful darkness hovered, mingling with a touch of something sinis-ter. 'Let's close ourselves in, like we used to,' she suggested. We pushed against the heavy timber door until the barn was almost pitch-black, and began to undress each other. 'This is heaven,' she whispered a few moments later. 'If only I could spend my whole life like this…'

Abruptly there were footsteps outside and the barn door was thrown wide. Yes, it was Kazia's father, the old, ever-coughing, ever-cursing Antek. He stood at the door with a large pitchfork in his hand. 'What are you doing, you little whore?' he snarled. 'And who is that son-of-a-bitch?' Within minutes the whole village — man, woman, child and dog — stood around us.

'It's a Jew, a Jew!' shouted a peasant. 'Let's take him to the Gestapo!'

'He is not!' Kazia cried. 'He's not!'

'Why the Gestapo?' said another peasant, who had a potato-nose and a moustache as big and bushy as a duster. 'Let's judge him ourselves. Maybe there is more than one Jew here, and if there is, there'll be plenty of vodka for all of us.'

This ingenious idea received general applause. I was chained to Rex, and instructed that I was to appear at first cock-crow before the magistrate at 13 Kowalska Street.

Suddenly it was sunrise. In front of the courthouse stood a guard with a three-headed dog. 'Room Z,' he announced. 'Follow the yellow line till you get there.' Although the court-house was a small insignificant-looking structure, its interior was enormous. I walked for hours through narrow, winding, unlit corridors, dingy passages and grey hallways. There were many doors but all were locked. Now and then a man's rough voice urged: 'If you walk faster, much faster, you might just get there before sunset.' At last I reached Room Z, a scarcely noticeable little turret. Its door had no number, just a sign: SPRAWIEDLIWOŚĆ (Justice). It was only later that I learnt that Justice and Z carried the same meaning here. I entered.

The courtroom, lit by candles, was packed to capacity. Behind a table covered in green sat the honourable magistrate: half man, half rooster. 'What's your name, loverboy?' he scoffed. 'And would you by any chance be Jewish?'

'No, he isn't, he isn't!' Kazia cried.

'We'll soon see. Drop your pants!'

'Żyd, Jude — Żyd, Jude,' chorused the whole assembly.

'Have you any relatives here?' asked the man-rooster, this time quite politely.

'Yes, your honour.'

'Then take me to them!'

I led the zealous procession through my Yiddish-speaking forest, all of us holding candles to light the way. Then, stopping in front of the royal oak, breathtaking in its majesty, I pointed to the sad crucifix in its branches. 'One of my relatives,' I said.

'I could hang you on the spot for such impertinence,' the magistrate thundered.

'Sir, you can check under his cloth if you like.'

My reply created a nervous rustle. The crowd grew visibly angry. 'Throw him into the jaws of Cerberus!' they screamed.

'Wait, hold it.' It was the village priest. 'The Gestapo doesn't accept leftovers,' he observed. 'Let's lock him up in Rex's kennel, and tomorrow, with God's help, we'll all be drinking vodka.'

At midnight Kazia crept in. After an embrace and a kiss, she murmured: 'Run for your life — run; run before it's too late.' Somehow I stood up and stepped out of the kennel. I ran. Shortly I reached the crossroads near the ghetto. The countryside was already in bloom; the grass was a lush young green, sprinkled with brilliant yellow wildflowers. An old man was standing there, old as time and youthful as a spark of dawn. Clad in night, he was dreaming a dream of light.

❧ *Final Departure* ❧

There was summer, with its flawless skies, and in the silence of dawn the thunder of heavy, distant guns. A wave of hallucinations gripped the ghetto. On sleepless nights some people watched and found Cassandra's face in the full moon; and all day long the disheartened gazed in horror to see hope writhing like a woman in travail. *O God almighty, let my tomorrow not miscarry, let life continue. Please, God, answer our prayers, for we are at the end of our tether.* The answer came swiftly next daybreak, on posters that had appeared overnight:

> Upon the highest authority, the Ghetto is to be evacuated to another location.
>
> Each factory, together with its families, is to travel to a new workplace.
> The first transport departs 3 August 1944.
> A quota of *5000 people* must be resettled daily.
> Luggage allowed: 15 to 20 kilograms maximum.
>
> The first transport will consist of all workers employed in clothing factory No. 1 at 45 Łagiewnicka Street, as well as those in factory No. 2 at 36 Łagiewnicka Street.
>
> Members of families of the abovementioned workers must attach themselves to the transport, to avoid families being torn asunder.
>
> Announcements of further transports will follow. Those designated to leave the Ghetto must appear at Radegast railway station not later than 7 a.m. on 3 August. The transport departs at 8 a.m.
>
> *Mordechai Chaim Rumkowski*
> *Eldest of the Jews in Litzmannstadt*

I quickly contacted and met with my underground cell leader, Bono. 'The news is not good,' he said. 'The first item on Radio Świt [meaning 'Daybreak'] reports that the chimneys of Auschwitz are smoking again. We have decided not to rise up, we don't have the means, we are alone.' His voice was dulled with disenchantment. 'Our attempt to make contact with our prewar comrades was unsuccessful. Hide as long as you can; the rest is up to fate.'

When I imparted the bitter tidings to my parents, mother let loose an almost animal howl. 'Don't you dare spread such awful news! People don't do things like this. We are going to work — hasn't Rumkowski ordered us to depart as a family, to take our bedding, our clothing and household goods to our new dwelling-places?'

Father stood there, a broken ruin of a man. I recalled Rumkowski's speech two years earlier, at the first resettlement of children and the elderly. 'It cannot be that they will tear babes from their mothers' breasts,' Chaim had said, 'and drag old fathers and mothers to some unknown place. The German is without mercy, he wages a terrible war, but he will not go as far as that in cruelty.' Next morning, however, the new day arrived with a deafening shrill:

This part of the Ghetto is to be liquidated today. Whoever is found here after 5 p.m. will be shot.

The area referred to — the district where my grandparents' grandparents had been born — was connected to the other, larger part of the ghetto by the timber footbridge that passed over Zgierska Street. This unexpected announcement contradicted the earlier statement about orderly evacuation of the ghetto. Panicking, we rushed wildly across the bridge that led to the other side of the ghetto. Amid the alarm, chaos and commotion I lost my family. I stopped for a moment, then ran back, hoping to spot them somewhere in the throng that had not yet managed to negotiate the bridge. But they had been carried away from me, like matches on the current of a surging river, towards the other end of the structure — where the Germans waited, whipping people like cattle into huge trucks that drove off without delay, to deliver them to the assembly point for departure.

I recall that sunny morning of shadows, violence, rapine and guile. The place of assembly for the condemned was firmly fenced in, so I couldn't see if anyone from my family was still there. At the gate stood an old German. I asked him if he would permit me to investigate. 'Yes,' he said. 'I can let you in, but I can't let you out.' I had a coin on me: heads they're there, tails they're not…

As I walked in, mother ran towards me with open arms. 'I knew it!' she exclaimed triumphantly to another German. 'I told you my son would come!'

Shortly after midday we boarded the train, but we did not depart until dusk. A hundred people were pressed into our feebly-lit wagon. It contained one small bucket for our human needs, which was quickly filled, and one barrel of water, which was quickly emptied. The heat was unbearable. Eventually the sickly light went out. Father, enveloped in darkness, stood in a corner like his own tombstone. Mother fretted over what we would do, we had no change of clothes. She didn't know that this was her last journey. My sister Pola cradled her whining Frumetl, and my sister Ida sang to her little Chayale, about how there was once a king…